SILVIO BERLUSCONI

TELEVISION, POWER
AND PATRIMONY

PAUL GINSBORG

V

VERSO

London • New York

First published by Verso 2004
© Paul Ginsborg 2004
All rights reserved

The moral rights of the author have been asserted

1 3 5 7 9 10 8 6 4 2

Verso
UK: 6 Meard Street, London W1F 0EG
USA: 180 Varick Street, New York, NY 10014—4606

Verso is an imprint of New Left Books

ISBN 1–84467–000–7

British Library Cataloguing in Publication Data
Ginsborg, Paul
   Silvio Berlusconi : television, power and patrimony
   1. Berlusconi, Silvio, 1936–   2. Television and politics –
   Italy   3. Television in politics – Italy   4. Television
   broadcasting – Italy
   I. Title
   302.2'345'0945

   ISBN 1844670007

Library of Congress Cataloging-in-Publication Data
Ginsborg, Paul
   Silvio Berlusconi : television, power and patrimony / Paul Ginsborg.
      p. cm
   ISBN 1-84467-000-7 (hardcover : alk. paper)
   1. Berlusconi, Silvio, 1936– 2. Italy—Politics and government—21st
century.   3. Television and politics—Italy.   4. Mass media—Political
aspects—Italy.   I. Title.
   DG583.8.B47G56 2004
   945.093'092—dc22

                                                              2003027792

Typeset in Perpetua by SetSystems, Saffron Walden, Essex
Printed in the USA by R.R. Donnelley & Sons

For my friends and colleagues of the Florentine
'Laboratorio per la democrazia'.

CONTENTS

Acknowledgements

My heartfelt thanks to Silvia Alessandri and Christian De Vito for their help in the preparation of this text.

Glossary

What follows below is a list of the official terms and institutions which appear most frequently in the book. For ease of reading, the vast majority of terms appear throughout in English.

Chief Procurator　**Procuratore capo**, the senior magistrate who directs the Office of Public Prosecution in every major city, and who assigns cases and responsibilities to the investigating magistrates of the same Office.

Christian Democrat party　**Democrazia cristiana**, a political party of Catholic inspiration, founded in 1942, dominant in Italian politics from 1946 until 1992. Heavily implicated in the corruption investigations of the 'Clean Hands' campaign (q.v.), the party dissolved in January 1994. Surviving fragments are present in both the coalitions of the centre-left and the centre-right.

'Clean Hands' campaign　**'Mani pulite'**, the popular name given to the series of judicial investigations launched in Milan in 1992, which uncovered a widespread network of corruption and illegal financing of political parties. The investigations led to charges being brought against many well-known Italian businessmen and politicians, some of whom were eventually sentenced by the courts.

CGIL   Confederazione generale italiana del lavoro, the oldest and largest of the Italian trade-union organisations, it now numbers some five and a half million members. The CGIL is left-wing in political orientation and its present general secretary is Guglielmo Epifani. The previous secretary was Sergio Cofferati, who held the post from 1994 to 2002.

CISL   Confederazione italiana sindacati lavoratori, the second largest trade-union organisation in the country, with just over four million members. Moderate and Catholic in orientation, its general secretary is Savino Pezzotta.

Constitutional Court   Corte costituzionale. Instituted in 1956, it has the task of ajudicating disputes relative to the constitutional legitimacy of laws. It is composed of fifteen judges.

Cassation Court   Corte di Cassazione, the third and highest level of the Italian judiciary system, dealing with all areas except constitutional ones. After the Court of Appeal (q.v.) has passed sentence in a case, both defence and prosecution have the right to appeal to the higher court, which rules on the legitimacy of sentences, but not on their merit.

Council of Ministers   Consiglio dei ministri, constituted by the President (q.v.) and ministers, who have varied in number in different phases of the Italian Republic's history. The present government of Silvio Berlusconi numbers twenty-three ministers.

Court of Appeal   Corte d'Appello, the second level of the Italian judicial system, to which either defence or prosecution may appeal for revision of a sentence passed by a lower court.

Chamber of Deputies   Camera dei deputati. The Chamber of Deputies and the Senate make up the Italian parliament. The Chamber has 630 deputies, elected for a five-year span.

Financial Police   Guardia di Finanza. This is a special corps which is dependent upon the Treasury Ministry but is also part of the armed forces of the state. Its principal tasks are the prevention and discovery of tax evasion, of contraband, and of financial violations of the law.

Fininvest. Since 1984 the overall name for Berlusconi's group of companies.

Forza Italia   Forza Italia. The political party created by Silvio Berlusconi in 1994, which gained 29.5 percent of the votes for the Chamber of Deputies (q.v.) in the national elections of 2001, and thus emerged as Italy's largest single political force.

Higher Council of the Magistracy   Consiglio superiore della magistratura. Instituted in 1958, the Council is the organ of self-government of the judiciary, and was envisaged by the Republican constitution of 1948 as a bulwark and safeguard of judicial autonomy. Its president is the President of the Republic (q.v.).

House of Liberties   Casa delle libertà, a coalition of centre-right forces (Forza Italia, the National Alliance, the Northern League, and the Catholic UDC) which won the national elections of May 2001.

Left Democrats   Democratici di sinistra (DS), the major party of the left, formed after the dissolution of the Italian Communist Party (PCI) in 1991. It polled 16.6 percent of the votes in the national election of 2001. Its secretary is Piero Fassino and president Massimo D'Alema.

Montecitorio   Palazzo di Montecitorio, a seventeenth-century palace in the heart of Rome, from 1871 the seat of the Chamber of Deputies.

National Alliance   Alleanza Nazionale, right-wing coalition and then party, founded in 1994, with the aim of transforming the neo-Fascist MSI (Movimento Sociale Italianao) into a more moderate force with wider electoral appeal. Its president is Gianfranco Fini, and it polled 12 percent of the vote in the national elections of 2001.

Northern League   Lega Nord, founded in 1991 by Umberto Bossi, a regionally based party which draws it support predominantly from Lombardy and Venetia. Anti-immigrant, it advocates strong regional autonomy and even advocated secession from the Italian state at one stage of its brief history. It polled 3.9 percent of the vote in 2001.

Olive Tree Coalition   L'Ulivo, a centre-left coalition of forces, first led by Romano Prodi, which narrowly won the national elections of 1996, but lost those of 2001.

Palazzo Chigi   Palazzo Chigi, a mainly seventeenth century palace, close to Montecitorio (q.v.), the official seat of the President of the Council of Ministers (q.v.).

President of the Council of Ministers Presidente del Consiglio dei Ministri, the head of Italian government, directs and coordinates the activities of the executive in the context of the powers granted by the Republican constitution. In this book sometimes referred to for convenience as 'premier' or 'prime minister'.

President of Regional Government Presidente della Regione, the head of the regional executive, wielding considerable and increasing power at the local level. Now sometimes called 'Governatore' (Governor), in recognition of this changing role.

President of the Republic Presidente della Repubblica, the head of the Italian state and the guardian of the Republican constitution. The powers of the President are limited but crucial, and to differing degrees Presidents have always played an active role in Italian politics. The President is elected by members of parliament for a seven-year term in office.

The Quirinale Palazzo del Quirinale, formerly the Papal residence, now the official seat of the President of the Republic, situated in the centre of Rome on the hill which bears the same name.

Rifondazione Comunista Partito della Rifondazione Comunista, literally 'the party for the refounding of Communism', formed in 1991 in the wake of the dissolution of the Italian Communist party, and in opposition to the more moderate Democratici di sinistra (q.v.). Its secretary is Fausto Bertinotti, and it gained 5.0 percent of the vote in the national elections of 2001.

Social Forums The World Social Forum is not an organisation, but 'an open meeting place for reflective thinking, democratic debate of ideas, formulation of proposals . . . by groups and movements of civil society that are opposed to neo-liberalism and to domination of the world by capital and any form of imperialism, and are committed to building a society centred on the human person' (from the WSF Charter of Principles).

UIL   Unione italiana del lavoro. Founded in 1949, it is the third force of Italian trade unionism with 1,900,000 members and occupies an intermediate position between the left-wing CGIL (q.v.) and the Catholic CISL (q.v.). Its general secretary is Luigi Angeletti.

List of Italian Presidents of the Council of Ministers and duration of their governments, 1983–2004

President	Date of nomination	Date of resignation
Bettino Craxi	4 August 1983	27 June 1986
Bettino Craxi	1 August 1986	3 March 1987
Amintore Fanfani	17 April 1987	28 April 1987
Giovanni Goria	28 July 1987	11 March 1988
Ciriaco De Mita	13 April 1988	19 May 1989
Giulio Andreotti	22 July 1989	29 March 1991
Giulio Andreotti	14 April 1991	24 April 1992
Giuliano Amato	28 June 1992	28 April 1993
Carlo Azeglio Ciampi	28 April 1993	16 April 1994
Silvio Berlusconi	10 May 1994	22 December 1994
Lamberto Dini	17 January 1995	11 January 1996
Romano Prodi	17 May 1996	9 October 1998
Massimo D'Alema	21 October 1998	18 December 1999
Massimo D'Alema	22 December 1999	19 April 2000
Giuliano Amato	25 April 2000	31 May 2001
Silvio Berlusconi	10 June 2001	

PROLOGUE

When I was a young researcher working in the Venetian archives, I once dared to ask a distinguished senior American professor who was sitting next to me what it had been like to be a historian in Italy at the time of Fascism. He looked at me benignly and replied: 'I didn't really notice.' It is even easier now not to notice. Everyday life continues as before, daily newspapers reflect a wide range of opinion, the sun shines, the tourists arrive, and we all eat extremely well. Yet something important is happening in Italy, potentially quite sinister, and the seeming normality of life serves to mask it very well.

Silvio Berlusconi's government of Italy since 2001, and his presidency of the European Union from July to December 2003, have given rise to much unease in international public opinion. The world's press has repeatedly posed a number of questions: does Berlusconi's combination of media and political power herald a new model of political control in modern democracy? Is his the most ambitious of the many populist answers to democracy's present fragility? And again, a question oft-repeated but which sounds historically ingenuous to many a sophisticated Italian ear: is history repeating itself, with Italy playing the same role as the precursor of Fascism as it did in the early 1920s?[1] After all, it was Primo Levi who wrote, as long ago as 1974, that 'every age has its Fascism'; and he went on to warn that 'one can reach such a condition in many ways, not necessarily by means of terror and police intimidation, but also by withholding or manipulating information, by polluting the judicial system and by paralysing the school system.'[2]

Others have preferred, either from conviction or convenience, to be sharply dismissive of Berlusconi. They point to the fact that his actions in government have been characterised mainly by improvisation, that he has no economic strategy, that he has been most concerned with the course of Italian justice directed against himself and his lawyer friend, Cesare Previti. The slight, accident-prone and clownish figure that he has cut on the European stage has only increased such suspicions. 'Burlesquoni' was how *The Economist* chose to dub him in the summer of 2003.[3]

Yet the cumulative evidence, culled not just from politics but from wider cultural processes, would suggest the need to take Silvio Berlusconi seriously. As of yet, there has been no theorisation of Berlusconi's project from the ranks of the Italian centre-right. He lacks a Giovanni Gentile, the distinguished philosopher who became Mussolini's Minister of Education, or even a Keith Joseph, able propagandist for Mrs. Thatcher. However, that does not imply that no project exists. One of the principal aims of this book is to assemble its constituent parts. By doing so, I hope to explain why Italy's

1 'The whole question lies in trying to estimate to what degree this Italian model, so preoccupying in itself, risks being extended in a tomorrow to other countries of Europe'; I.Ramonet, 'Berlusconi', *Le Monde diplomatique*, February 2002, p. 1.

2 Article from *Corriere della Sera*, 8 May 1974, reprinted in P.Levi, *Opere*, vol. I, Turin 1997, p. 1187.

3 Charlemagne, 'Burlesquoni', *The Economist*, 12 July 2003, p. 29.

present experience has a significance that goes far beyond the narrow and complicated realm of the country's politics.

Of course, Berlusconi may well fail. One of the hazards for a historian who chooses to analyse a historical process in full flow is that he or she cannot enjoy the habitual professional privilege of knowing how the story finishes. How much easier it was to write about the Venetian revolution of 1848–49, knowing before I begun how it had ended! None the less, I shall try not to hedge my bets. I believe that Italian history in these years, whatever its final destiny, is highly instructive for a number of central issues in the modern world: the nature of personal dominion at a time of crisis in representative democracy; the relationship between the media system and political power; the connection between consumerism, families and politics; finally, the ongoing weakness of the Left, its failure to identify and combat dangers, its incapacity to arouse enthusiasm for credible alternatives.

Old concepts and new protagonists

The coalition of centre-right parties which won the last Italian general elections in 2001 was called '*La Casa delle Libertà*', the 'House of Liberties'. In fact, perusing the two volumes of Silvio Berlusconi's speeches which cover the period 1994–2000, one is struck by how much space is dedicated therein to the concept of liberty, and how little to that of democracy.[4] The liberty that Berlusconi has in mind is prevalently 'negative', a classic freeing from interference or impedi-

---

4 *Discorsi per la democrazia* and *L'Italia che ho in mente*, Milan 2000. There is, of course, a great deal of political and intellectual posturing in these interventions, which often bear little relation to the actual practice of Berlusconi's governing party, Forza Italia. This is particularly true of Berlusconi's prepared speeches to parliament (*Discorsi per la democrazia*).

ment. Individuals have to be placed in that condition of freedom which allows them, in an expression borrowed from the Risorgimento, to '*fare da sé*' (to 'go it alone'), to express fully their individuality. Economy and society have likewise to be liberated, 'from oppressive chains, from the weight of bureaucracy and suffocating procedures, and from fiscal pressure which has grown too fast and too far.'[5] Competition increases such liberty: 'Every one must be free to offer his own goods, services and ideas to his peers, who can decide freely whether to accept or reject them. Every limitation to competition is equivalent to the violation of the freedom and rights of everyone.'[6] All this will have a familiar ring to Anglo-American ears.

'Positive freedom', on the other hand, receives scant attention. For Berlusconi, the market spontaneously creates a work ethic, as well as the moral principles of loyalty and honesty. By contrast, the State, however much it tries, cannot legislate values into being. Rather it is to be regarded with suspicion every time it seeks to do so, or when it tries to limit free competition in the name of the collectivity. Behind such intervention there always lurks 'the interests of certain groups and classes, whose electoral support is sought by those who hold power.'[7] Anything other than a 'minimum State' is a potential threat to the person of the citizen: 'We cannot accept their desire to control everything, their invasion of our lives, their presumption to regulate all our activities!'[8]

As for democracy, when Berlusconi does pay some attention to it, his discourse is nearly always confined to the need for regular elections, and for the electorate to have the right to vote directly for

5 'Discourse to the Senate' in *Discorsi per la democrazia*, 16 May 1994, p. 22.

6 'Speech to the National Congress of the Forza Italia Youth Movement' in *L'Italia che ho in mente*, 11 December 1999, p. 114.

7 Ibid., pp. 114–17.

8 'Speech at Vicenza', *L'Italia che ho in mente*, 26 November 1998, p. 201.

single personalities – the president of the Council of Ministers; the presidents of the Regions; ideally for the president of the Republic. His is a vision which concentrates on regularity and personality. What is never considered, and this should come as no surprise, is the wider communicative and cultural context in which regular elections occur, or the differing resources available to individual candidates to influence their outcome. There is no idea of a level playing field. Likewise, scant attention is paid to the benign consequences of a balance of powers within the democratic state. Judicial autonomy is regarded with anathema.

Berlusconi's view of politics is thus based on the corrosive combination of negative freedom and formal personalised democracy. The combination is corrosive because negative freedom unaccompanied by its positive counterpart fatally undermines the attempt to assert collective interests. It denies the possibility for a given community to establish, in the name of a collective good, a sense of limit, a necessary framework in which the search for self-realisation needs to take place.[9] It encourages instead the creation in civil society of over-powerful individuals unwilling to submit to a much weakened general rule of law. They are free, too free one might suggest, to *'fare da sé'*.

At the same time the rules of democracy, limited to the questions of regularity and personality, do nothing to guarantee an equitable

9 The classic text on negative and positive freedom is of course that of Isaiah Berlin, 'Two concepts of liberty' [1958], in *Four Essays on Liberty*, London 1969. The possibilities of authoritarianism implicit in positive freedom were always uppermost in Berlin's mind, perhaps exaggeratedly so; whereas it seems important to insist, as Charles Taylor has done, that 'freedom resides at least in part in collective control over the common life'; see his 'What's wrong with negative liberty', in Alan Ryan (ed.), *The Idea of Freedom: Essays in Honour of Isaiah Berlin*, Oxford 1979, p. 175. For a recent and powerful revisiting of this debate, and the suggestion of a third concept of liberty as absence of dependence, see Quentin Skinner, 'A third concept of liberty', in *Proceedings of the British Academy*, vol. 117, 2001 Lectures, Oxford 2003.

terrain on which elections can be held. On the contrary. Few, if any, restrictions exist to impede new agents emergent from the tertiary sector, particularly from telecommunications, finance and entertainment, from using their very considerable economic and mediatic resources to influence heavily, and sometimes to storm, the democratic sphere. The way is open for the creation of modern patrimonial figures.[10] They have little natural sense of democracy, still less a sense of limits. They are driven, rather, by fierce acquisitive instincts, by family ambitions and clan loyalties, by an iron sense of their own self-importance.

~

How far such figures are able to make progress depends upon the state of health of the democratic system at a national and international level. Their advent has occurred at a time when representative democracy is superficially triumphant on a global scale. In the year 2000, 120 out of the 192 countries of the United Nations were defined as democratic. Twelve years earlier, only 66 nations out of the then total of 167 had qualified as such.[11] Yet democracy has demonstrated in the years of its triumph a new fragility: falling numbers of voters; widespread cynicism about its politicians and even its institutions; crumbling mass parties. Its expansion on a global scale has thus been accompanied by crisis in its homelands.[12] However much democracy is an intimate and striking

10 For an extended discussion of this patrimonialism, see below, ch. 5, pp. 116–22.

11 L. Diamond and M. Plattner, 'Introduction', in Id. (eds), *The Global Divergence of Democracies*, Baltimore 2001, p. x, table 1.

12 For the considerable literature on these themes, see amongst others David Beetham (ed.), *Defining and Measuring Democracy*, London 1994; M.J.Sandel, *Democracy's Discontent: America in Search of a Public Philosophy*, Cambridge, Mass. 1996; as well as the ensuing discussion, Anita L. Allen and Milton C.Regan, Jr., (eds), *Debating Democracy's Discontent*, Oxford 1998; Susan Pharr and Robert D. Putnam (eds), *Disaffected Democracies: What's Troubling the Trilateral Countries?*, Princeton 2000; Robert D.Putnam, (ed.), *Democracies in Flux*, Oxford 2002.

feature of modernity, it has no inevitable dynamic of forward march, nor inbuilt quality control.

Outside the narrow political sphere, often isolated in antiquated and protracted rituals, the economic, social and cultural transformations of the last twenty years have been great indeed. They press upon politics, influencing and even moulding it. The centrality of the media is here to stay, bending politics to its own logic, its own sense of time, its own commodity-driven needs. The media, dominated by television, do not just personify and simplify democratic politics, thus distorting its contents. Their markets, extremely oligarchical in character, throw up personalities of the sort that are under consideration here.

Of course, media moguls have existed before, as has preoccupation concerning their overarching influence. After the First World War the power of newspaper barons in Britain and their control of the popular press were considered by many a threat to democracy. The critic Norman Angell wrote in 1922:

> What England thinks is largely controlled by a very few men, not by virtue of the direct expression of any opinion of their own, but by controlling the distribution of emphasis in the telling of facts: so stressing one group of them and keeping another group in the background as to make a given conclusion inevitable.[13]

In the same year Walter Lippmann had warned his readers tersely that 'news and truth are not the same thing.'[14] However, the influence of

13 Norman Angell, *The Press and the Organisation of Society*, London 1922, p. 26; quoted in John Eldridge, Jenny Kitzinger and Kevin Williams, *The Mass Media and Power in Modern Britain*, Oxford 1997, p. 29. For contemporary newspaper barons, Nicholas Coleridge, *Paper Tigers*, London 1993.

14 Walter Lippmann, *Public Opinion*, New York 1922, p. 358. He went on (p. 363): 'At its best the press is a servant and guardian of institutions; at its worst, it is a means by which a few exploit social disorganisation to their own ends'.

the print media can with difficulty be compared to the constant presence of television in modern homes. Berlusconi, as we shall see, is a broadcasting tycoon, not a newspaper baron. The process by which modern consumerism, commercial television and political power are being linked is an entirely new one.

The historical realities of such a process are, at least so far, complicated and far from linear. In the biographies of the powerful media figures that have emerged in these years to invade the public sphere, a number of elements reoccur, not always in the same combination: initial fortunes made in the building trade or in financial speculation; the spectacular transformation of ailing firms or media enterprises; acquisition of, and investment in, sporting clubs with considerable popular followings; 'creative' financing and other market operations which border on, or go beyond, the limits of legality; and, of course, the central role of commercial television in launching political careers.

The connections between media and politics are not always the same. I shall be concentrating here upon ownership and wealth as the basis of power, but there are, obviously, other variants. Some of the great media entrepreneurs, including the most powerful of all, Rupert Murdoch, choose to wield political influence indirectly. They are distinctly patrimonial figures (Murdoch has ambitions for ownership and control which extend to all five continents), but hardly charismatic. Others have risen and fallen with startling rapidity, overreaching themselves and accumulating insurmountable debt. Jean-Marie Messier constructed Vivendi, a huge media empire, in very few years, only to see it crumble before his eyes. The ill-fated Bernard Tapie in Marseilles and the embattled Michael Bloomberg in New York both used local politics as a power base, without conspicuous success. Roberto Marinho, through the powerful TV Globo network in Brazil, successfully took his young candidate Fernando Collor de Mello to the presidency of Brazil in 1989, only to see him squander power in record time. Cem Uzan in Turkey, the founder of the country's first pay television, Star TV, tried recently to assert himself on a national political level, but with limited success. Thaksin Shinawatra, on the other hand, the proprietor of a significant telecommunications empire in Thailand, became the country's Prime Minister in January, 2001, just two months before Berlusconi triumphed in Italy.[15]

Trajectories vary, as does the degree of political and legal constraint exercised upon the freedom of action of the new tycoons. The antibodies which democracy offers vary from country to country. In some cases Lilliputian prosecuting magistrates have hung on to these colossi with grim determination, tying flimsy ropes around their legs and causing them eventually to topple over. In others, the long-term political culture of a region has favoured their rise. Southern Europe, South-East Asia, Turkey and South America, where politics, even in their democratic form, have been dominated by deep-rooted clientelism and where the rule of law has often been uncertain, are natural terrains for such figures.[16] But their rise to power and influence is not limited to such settings. There is a growing list of American billionaire politicians – Ross Perot, Steve Forbes, Mike Bloomberg, Jon Corzine, the senator from New Jersey – who have spent their way into office by buying unprecedented amounts of TV time. In the presidential

15 For Thaksin Shinawatra's victory, see 'Tycoon or Thai Con?', *The Economist*, 11 January 2001; for Cem Uzan, www.metimes.com/cem_uzan.htm; for Collor de Mello, Venicio A. de Lima, 'Brazilian television in the 1989 presidential election: constructing a president', in Thomas E. Skidmore (ed.), *Television, Politics and the Transition to Democracy in Latin America*, Washington D.C. 1993, pp. 97–117; for Tapie, Christophe Bouchet, *Tapie, l'homme d'affaires*, Paris 1994; for Messier, Jo Johnson and Martine Orange, *The Man Who Tried to Buy the World*, London 2003. A useful introduction, though now a little dated, is Jeremy Tunstall and Michael Palmer, *Media Moguls*, London 1991.

16 A fundamental treatment of this theme, covering the Balkans and Latin America, though not Italy, is N.P. Mouzelis, *Politics in the Semi-Periphery*, London 1986.

campaign of 1996, Perot broke all the rules by buying half-hour 'infomercials' on commercial television, and was rewarded with 18.9 percent of the vote.[17] Where de-regulation is the name of the game, and politics is highly personalised, the space for manoeuvre is correspondingly great.

Silvio Berlusconi represents the Italian declination of these trends. His is the most ambitious attempt to date to combine media control and political power. He is the first of these figures to lead a major nation state, ranked seventh in the world in economic terms. We may choose to regard him as a prototype or as an exception, and time will tell which of these views is closer to the truth. In either case, his trajectory is significant and worthy of being studied in depth.

17 See the interesting comparison by Enrico Canaglia, *Berlusconi, Perot e Collor come political outsider*, Soveria Mannelli 2000, pp. 51–93; also the comments of Alexander Stille, 'Italy: the family business', *The New York Review of Books*, vol. 50, no. 15, 9 October 2003.

1: BUILDINGS

1. First steps

Milan, the city in which Silvio Berlusconi was born on 29 September 1936, has always occupied a special place in Italian history. In March 1848, its inhabitants staged an extraordinary urban insurrection, one of the most significant events of the Risorgimento. After five days of sustained fighting, they threw out of the city the garrison of 13,000 troops commanded by the redoubtable Austrian, Field Marshal Radetzky. In the decades after the unification of Italy, the city became known as the 'moral capital' of Italy, industrious and dynamic, the country's commercial and financial centre, in contrast to Rome, the centre of politics and of intrigue, as well as of the Catholic Church.[1] The Milanese bourgeoisie, closely connected geographically to the rest of Europe, to Switzerland and Germany in particular, was robust and in part enlightened. It was capable of cultural expression at the highest European level, as the history of its music temple, La Scala, bore witness. When the young Milanese Futurist painter Umberto Boccioni took Paris by storm in February 1912, he wrote home: 'The whole

---

1 G.Rosa, *Il mito della capitale morale*, Turin 1982.

battle has revolved around my "States-of-mind" paintings. . . . The French are astonished that from a small provincial city like Milan there has emerged a word [Futurism] which has quite taken them aback, accustomed even as they are to novelties of the most absurd sort.'[2]

After the First World War, Milan was the first reference point for Benito Mussolini when he founded his Fascist movement. The city, all energy and movement, money making and pragmatism, Italian but not Mediterranean, has always been divided: between reform and reaction, between integrative and repressive strategies towards its numerous working class, between radical innovation (as in the world of design), and dull provincial conservatism. The biography of Silvio Berlusconi can be read as the story of one part of the Milanese bourgeoisie, dynamic, parvenu and without a sense of limit, as it gains ascendancy over the other, and in the end transforms it.

Berlusconi was born on the city's northern extremity, in the quarter called Isola Garibaldi, 'Garibaldi's Island', where in 1936 the city ended and the fields began, and where today the city still ends but the urban agglomeration continues. His father Luigi, twenty-eight-years-old at the time of Silvio's birth, was a clerk in the Rasini bank, more a credit boutique than a bank, with just one branch in Piazza Mercanti. His mother, Rosella Bossi, from a lower-middle-class background, was twenty-five and a housewife. She was always to be the dominant force in the family. Silvio was the first child, born the year in which Italian troops entered Adis Abeba and Mussolini proclaimed his colonial empire. Two other children were to follow: Antonietta in 1943, and Paolo in 1949.

For the Berlusconi family, the war years were dramatic but not

2 Umberto Boccioni, Gli scritti editi e inediti, Milan 1971, p. 346, letter to Nino Barbantini.

catastrophic. In 1943, Rossella, pregnant with her second child, and Silvio were evacuated to near Como to escape the Allied air raids on the city. Like many young Milanese, Silvio's father Luigi chose not to respond to Mussolini's call to enrol in the army of the Republic of Salò, but rather to seek refuge in Switzerland. Silvio, seven at the time, was not to see his father again for nearly two years. He suffered this absence very much, but it may well have served to strengthen those elements of independence, pride and determination which form so central a part of his character. It also meant that the family culture which he imbibed in these formative years was not a die-hard Fascist one, but still less did it have the Resistance as its reference point. Faced with the difficult choices of allegiance during those years – to Mussolini and the Germans, to the Resistance and the Allies, or to no one in particular – choices upon which the destinies of entire family groups depended, the Berlusconi family chose exit rather than loyalty.[3]

After the war Silvio's parents sent him to a boarding college run by the priests of the Salesian order, the Sant'Ambrogio in Via Copernico, near the central station. Theirs was an ambitious and radical choice, unusual for an Italian family. The boys boarding there were allowed home for very few days during the school year, and this protracted absence from home was only in part compensated for by long summer holidays. The Salesiani were strict and the school had a good reputation. The day began at seven A.M. with breakfast and Mass, there were lessons until lunch (Italian, Latin, Greek, mathematics, history, philosophy, music and religious education), the Rosary afterwards, and then more lessons until supper. Lights went out at nine P.M. in the long austere dormitories, each containing more than

---

3 For a compelling account of the need to choose, see ch. 1 of Claudio Pavone, *Una guerra civile*, Milan 1980. On exit and loyalty, Albert O.Hirschman, *Shifting Involvements*, Princeton 1982.

fifty beds. Berlusconi stayed at the Sant'Ambrogio from 1948 to 1955, from the age of eleven to eighteen. His school records show him to have been an excellent student who obtained high grades, though never the maximum for good behaviour. If he had a weakness, at least in terms of the school's own hierarchy of values, it was a lack of profound religious conviction. One of his companions remembers that 'during prayers, [Silvio] lost concentration. His lips moved mechanically, without forming the words, his thoughts were clearly elsewhere.'[4] In spite of his rigorous Catholic education, Berlusconi was never going to be a Christian Democrat, an Aldo Moro or Giulio Andreotti, figures who combined intense personal ambition with profound religious conviction and who were the dominant force in reshaping Italy in these postwar years. Berlusconi was always a 'lay' figure, attracted to the world of business, not politics, to all that moved and was modern, not to the canons and rituals as well as the timeless serenity of Italian Catholicism.

There are many anecdotes about him at the Sant'Ambrogio. One of the most repeated is that of him selling his rapidly completed homework to his companions for sweets or little objects, but preferably for money. His father remembered once asking his son, who was fifteen at the time, how he spent the five hundred lira he gave him each week. Silvio refused to reply, and when his father left him the money as usual on the sideboard, he refused to take it: 'The episode', recounted Luigi Berlusconi, 'encapsulates all that my son is: his pride, his independence, his stubbornness.' And he added, almost fearfully, 'If you touch his pride, then it's curtains [*addio*].'[5]

At school Silvio made a friend, Fedele Confaloniere, who was to

---

4 Giovanni Ruggeri and Mario Guarino, *Berlusconi. Inchiesta sul signor TV*, Milan 1994, p. 22. The testimony is that of Giulio Colombo.

5 Giorgio Ferrari, *Il padrone del diavolo. Storia di Silvio Berlusconi*, Milan 1990, p. 7.

stay by his side in all the years to come, and who is the current President of Mediaset, Berlusconi's television company. He was in the year below Silvio, but they shared a great passion for music. Confaloniere had attended Milan's prestigious Conservatory and played the piano since he was four years old; Berlusconi sang along and played the double bass. He adored Gilbert Bécaud, Yves Montand, Nat King Cole and Frank Sinatra. By the age of sixteen, the two boys were organising their first, improvised concerts during the summer holidays, and later, at university, they were to play in various nightclubs. One of Silvio's first jobs was as a *chanteur* and compère on cruise ships in the Mediterranean. He recounted that often single-handedly he had to keep large groups entertained all evening with jokes, songs, and so on. Bernard Tapie, born in a Paris suburb in 1942, who was to mirror many of the earlier elements of Berlusconi's rise to fame, was also to try his hand at a singing career. He, like Berlusconi, was endowed with considerable charm, and even recorded one or two 45s.[6] But neither of them had any lasting success in this field.

It is worth comparing these early years of Berlusconi with those of another major figure in the cohort of modern media tycoons. Rupert Murdoch, born in 1931, is five years Berlusconi's senior. He was the son of an influential Australian newspaper owner, Keith Murdoch, who was knighted in 1933, and who owned the *Melbourne Herald* and *Weekly Times* group. Murdoch was thus born into the art and was to enjoy a considerable inheritance from which to construct his empire. Berlusconi, and Tapie, began from nothing. Just as Berlusconi's formative years were unusually internal and confined, so Murdoch's were extraordinarily external, free, even wild. In 1938 Murdoch's father bought a sheep station on the Murrumbidgee River near Wagga Wagga, some 16,000 acres in all, mainly rolling rocky hills. Rupert

6 Bouchet, *Tapie*, pp. 23ff.

and his elder sister, Helen, would ride all day, or catch rabbits, hares and water rats. Rupert sold the water rats for their skins, six pence each. Helen, who had done the skinning, received from him one penny per skin.[7]

Both men went to university. Berlusconi enrolled at the State University of Milan, where he studied Law. Murdoch went to Oxford to read, nominally, history. Berlusconi's father asked his son to maintain himself while at university, which he did in a variety of ways. Murdoch enjoyed one of the best sets of rooms in Worcester College and was one of the few undergraduates to sport a car. In 1953, coached frantically by Asa Briggs, he got a third-class degree. Berlusconi graduated, slowly but well, in 1961, with a thesis of considerable relevance to his future, on the contractual aspects of advertising slots.[8] He obtained the highest vote possible, and his thesis received a prize from the Manzoni advertising agency.

2. The construction industry

Milan in the early 1960s was a city which offered many possibilities to determined young graduates, even those who had trained in the law. Differently from many other moments in Italy's postwar history, the labour market was a flexible one and in the North there was nearly full employment. The 'economic miracle', as it was called at the time, was in the process of making Italy one of the world's richest economies. Membership of the recently established European Common Market, a good transport system, design flair, entrepreneurial

---

7 William Shawcross, *Murdoch. The Making of a Media Empire*, 2nd revised ed., New York 1997, pp. 17–29.

8 In the Italian university system there is no obligation on the student to complete a first degree within three years, as is habitually the case in Britain.

skills, and above all the availability of great quantities of cheap labour from the South were the elements which combined to produce an unprecedented boom. One example of the industrial transformation will have to suffice here. In 1951, Italy was producing just 18,500 fridges a year; by 1967 this figure had reached 3.2 million, making the country the third largest producer of fridges in the world, after the United States and Japan.

Milan expanded rapidly. There was money to be made not only from the factories, but in the construction industry as well. This was the path chosen by Silvio Berlusconi. His problem was not a shortage of imagination or determination, but a chronic lack of initial capital. For the first four blocks of flats he constructed, in via Alciati (1961–62), he persuaded the head of his father's bank, Carlo Rasini, to stand guarantee for him. As for the potential purchasers of the flats, he convinced them to put down deposits on homes that existed only on paper. This was not an uncommon practice in Milan at the time since demand for housing far exceeded the supply. Berlusconi revealed himself a master of persuasion, and of attention to detail. Legend has it that the first flat was sold to the mother of his great friend and musical companion, Fedele Confalonieri. She was convinced, wrongly as it turned out, that there would be no room for a garage. Her son commented later:

> From his early days Berlusconi took calculated risks. Later on, he was at his best in motivating and guiding other men. Above all, his natural inclination has always been to keep initial costs to a minimum, to exploit to the maximum a wide network of contacts, to make alliances with those who have something to gain from an undertaking, and in particular to listen to and get on the same wavelength as his clients.[9]

9 Ferrari, *Il padrone*, p. 15.

After Via Alciati, it was time for something more ambitious. At Brugherio, just outside Milan, Berlusconi planned a complex of apartment buildings to accommodate approximately 4,000 people. He founded a new company, Edilnord S.p.a, and sought sponsors for his project. The Rasini bank supported him again, but the other principal source of finance was a murkier one: a Swiss company, the Finanzierungsgesellschaft für Residenzen Ag of Lugano, whose real proprietors have never been identified. The ambitious operation was at high risk. In 1964 market conditions were less favourable than three years earlier, interest rates were higher, and Brugherio was too isolated. Yet Berlusconi made a success of this project as well. He persuaded a key pension-fund manager to buy up flats in block,[10] whole page advertisements were taken in the *Corriere della Sera*, by 1969 the one thousand flats had been sold.[11]

The third building project, Milano 2 (1970–79), was the one which made Berlusconi's name. Milano 2 was an early Italian exercise in bounded space. It was located in the commune of Segrate, east of Milan, not far distant from the Linate airport. An enclosed residential complex for some 10,000 people, it was guarded by means of an elaborate system of concierges and night watchmen.[12]

The homes of Milano 2 were designed for the well-to-do Milanese bourgeoisie, both traditional and dynamic, young and old. Indeed, Italian families' preference for emotional and spatial proximity, for close daily contact between grandparents, parents, and children, meant that the project had to appeal to different age groups. It was sold as a city 'for number ones,' but also as a place where you could have 'a house in Milan without the smog and traffic jams of Milan',

10 For further details of this encounter, see below, ch. 5, p. 126.

11 G.Fiori, *Il venditore*, Milan 1995, pp. 32–4.

12 The best description in English of Milano 2 is in John Foot, *Milan since the Miracle*, Oxford 2001, pp. 100–1.

and enjoy 'a countryside house in the city.' Its dominant ethos reflected, but also helped to promote, the metamorphosis of Milanese capitalism in the late 1970s and early 1980s. This was the beginning of the era of the 'Milano da bere', the 'city you can drink', a city of new wealth founded upon telecommunications, finance, fashion and advertising.[13]

In its architectural design, Milano 2 can best be described as a cosy reaction to modernism. Its architects (Ragazzi, Hoffer and Pozza) preferred red brick to concrete, shunned away from high rise and surrounded homes with green spaces and ever-green trees. The complex boasts as its central axis a porticoed street one and a half kilometres in length, offering a very wide range of shops. Pedestrians, cyclists, and motorists are kept carefully separate. The central piazza overlooks a small artificial lake. Every Friday Berlusconi toured the building site, and Fedele Confalonieri remembers the apprehension of his team and his friend's 'extraordinary sense of detail and of the particular.'[14]

The real strength of Milano 2 lay with the quality of services it offered: a hotel and a conference centre, six schools, a church, a running track and swimming pools, underground parking and cable television. This last offered six channels, three for the RAI, the Italian public service, and two for abroad. The last, free channel was used, on the instigation of some of the residents, as a local news station for Milano 2 itself. TeleMilano, as it was called, was born in 1974. At first Berlusconi regarded it as an amusing optional extra, but it was to be the beginning of his television empire.

13 'Milano da bere' was an advertising slogan for an after-dinner drink, Amaro Ramazzotti. For its significance as the dominant image of the city in the 1980s, see Foot, *Milan*, pp. 165–7.

14 Ferrari, *Il padrone*, p. 38. See also Paolo Madron, *Le gesta del Cavaliere*, Milan 1994, pp. 21–2.

Berlusconi is fond of recalling how difficult the completion of Milano 2 was: 'When my morale is low, I put my hands in my pockets and go for a walk in Milano 2. I remember how many people were against me . . . Theirs was a political and bureaucratic machine perfectly designed to impede, to prohibit, to delay and to hinder.'[15] Berlusconi had to liberate Milano 2 from this machine, to assert the right of freedom from interference that was central to his success. He had to stop the 'Communist magistrates', as he called them, from controlling the regularity of the building contracts, the trade unions from making a fuss about working conditions, architectural professors and the newspapers from criticising the quality of the project. He had also to persuade the airport authorities at Linate to change the flight paths of the incoming and outgoing jets so as not to disturb the new residents.

3. Horses for courses

All this persuasion and desistance not only had a price, but raised larger questions about business practices, public ethics and the rule of law. In his valuable biography of Silvio Berlusconi, published in 1995, the journalist Giuseppe Fiori listed his subject's principal character traits.[16] He paid tribute to Berlusconi's courage, talent, and creativity, his optimism and exceptional work capacity, his desire to please and attention to the charming gesture. He noted his subject's stubbornness and volubility, as well as his boundless desire to make a name for himself. He could not fail to underline Berlusconi's ambiguity and

15 S.E.D'Anna and G.Moncalvo (eds), *Berlusconi in Concert* [in Italian], London 1994, p. 316.

16 Fiori's *Antonio Gramsci. Life of a Revolutionary* was published by New Left Books in 1970.

'*spregiudicatezza*', or lack of scruples, his deft footwork in the world of secret deals and his sense of clan.[17]

It might well be argued that such characteristics were necessary elements of being a building trade entrepreneur in Milan in the 1970s. Certainly it was habitual practice, and not just in that particular place and time, to surround oneself with capable lawyers, see how the law could be bent in one's favour, and pay little attention to questions of public responsibility. If ethics and economic activity had once been firmly linked – in the eighteenth century the academic discipline of economics had been considered a branch of ethics, and Adam Smith had been professor of moral philosophy at the University of Glasgow – the two had moved far apart by the end of the twentieth century. Business is business. As *The Economist* declared recently with commendable frankness: 'Businesses are ultimately interested in one thing: profits . . . If businesses think that treating their customers and staff well, or adopting a policy of "corporate social responsibility", or using ecologically friendly stationery will add to their profits, they will do it. Otherwise they will not.'[18] It was to take Mediaset, Berlusconi's television holding company, more than twenty years before it started producing a minimum of 'socially responsible advertising' amongst the tens of thousands of advertising spots that it broadcasts regularly.[19]

However, at the beginning of Berlusconi's career the question was not so much one of public ethics and responsibility, as of the necessary sense of limits and of transparency imposed by the law. Here the shadows cast by his early decisions have never really left him. Either something in his family and school education, or else the extreme gap

17 Fiori, *Il venditore*, p. 41. For a long discussion of '*spregiudicatezza*', see Perry Anderson, 'Land without scruple', *London Review of Books*, vol. 24, no. 6, 21 March 2002.

18 See the survey, 'Globalisation and its critics', in *The Economist*, 29 September 2001, p. 4.

19 It is called 'Comunicazione sociale Mediaset'.

between the size of his ambition and the shortage of his capital, or else the collective ethos of the group of friends with whom he built his empire, or perhaps all three, pushed him in directions that were later to be much criticised and the subject of legal actions.

The financing of Milano 2, and its successor Milano 3, has remained a great mystery. For the early flats of Via Alciati, Berlusconi's sources of capital and partners were, legally speaking, clearly visible. For Milano 2 they are buried in a jungle of purely nominal proprietors, offshore companies, financial Chinese boxes. Berlusconi's name 'disappears' on 29 September 1968 and only surfaces again seven years later, in 1975. What can be the reasons for such an extensive and temporally protracted dissimulation?[20]

The accusations, which have been repeatedly made in Italy, are that Berlusconi used money from highly suspect sources to finance his early operations and that he employed such capital in complicated and questionable circular flows of funds. There were various possible sources of finance. One such was capital which had been illegally exported from Italy (at the time all such movements were strictly controlled), and then channelled back from Swiss bank accounts towards Italy's stock exchange, which is in Milan not Rome.

Another possibility was laundered money from the Mafia. The magistrate Paolo Borsellino, in one of his last interviews before being killed by the Mafia at Palermo in July 1992, explained to French television the origins of so much liquidity:

20 Between 1978 and 1985 *The Economist* has estimated that some 93.9 billion lira, of unknown origin, flowed into the twenty-two companies of Berlusconi's empire; 'Silvio Berlusconi. An Italian Story', *The Economist*, 28 April 2001, p. 23. For the shareholder loans of 1977–78, see 'An open letter to Silvio Berlusconi', *The Economist*, 2 August 2003, especially section 6, 'Your early business career', available on http://www.Economist. See also Fiori, *Il venditore*, p. 39, as well as Ruggeri and Guarino, *Berlusconi*, pp. 45–66. The first edition of Ruggeri and Guarino's book, dating back to 1987, was the subject of an unsuccessful libel action by Silvio Berlusconi.

At the beginning of the 1970s, Cosa Nostra became a firm, in the sense that it took over the drug trade in such a massive way as to make of it a monopoly. Cosa Nostra thus began to manage an enormous amount of money for which it obviously sought outlets. Its capital was exported and deposited in safe bank accounts abroad, and certain of its members entered into contact with financiers expert in the movement of capital.[21]

One of Milan's most famous stockbrokers, Aldo Ravelli, referred to the Mafia as one of the three great sections of the Italian bourgeoisie, at least in terms of its financial resources.[22]

From an early period in Berlusconi's business career there existed a significant Sicilian connection, though not necessarily a Mafia one. In personal terms, it took the form of his long collaboration with Marcello Dell'Utri, who was born in Palermo in 1941. The two had met at university in Milan. Berlusconi was just finishing as Dell'Utri began, and the latter, lonely and rather intimidated by the great northern capital, was always to be grateful to Berlusconi for his instant friendship. The relationship was not as profound or as harmonious as that with Fedele Confalonieri; Dell'Utri was to feel more than once that his talents were not being sufficiently appreciated. But he recognised in Berlusconi some sort of father figure.[23] He

21 The interview, of 21 May 1992, is published in full in E.Veltri and M.Travaglio, *L'odore dei soldi*, Rome 2001, pp. 47–50. The quote is on pp. 49–50.

22 See his extended and illuminating conversation with F.Tamburini, *Misteri d'Italia*, Milan 1996, which Ravelli allowed to be published only after his death, p. 183. His insider's typology of the Italian bourgeoisie was not a flattering one. Section one was a 'semi-clean' bourgeoisie, headed by Agnelli; section two was 'intent on gaining quota at any cost, without scruples and often outside the law'; section three was the Mafia. Two and three, according to Ravelli, were often intertwined.

23 See the interrogation of Dell'Utri at the Tribunale di Torino, 5 October 1996, where he was questioned about the legal case he took out against Fininvest, and how the resentment that lay behind it was dissolved by Berlusconi: 'Then Berlusconi, how can I

also said on one occasion, rather revealingly, that Berlusconi could pardon dishonesty but not stupidity.[24]

In 1974 Berlusconi took a symbolic step of some significance, one that was to play a central part in the construction of his image. He bought the great and beautiful eighteenth-century villa of San Martino at Arcore, north of Milan, the historic country home of the noble Casati Stampa di Soncino family. It has 147 rooms. By buying Arcore, Berlusconi clearly signalled the grandiosity of his ambitions and their patrimonial nature. Not for him the austerity of Enrico Cuccia, Milan's and Italy's most influential banker, who was said to have lived like a bank clerk and had set the tone for one part of the Milanese bourgeoisie ever since the war. In the park surrounding the villa of San Martino, Berlusconi constructed an imposing mausoleum to house the bodily remains not only of his own family, but those of his closest friends as well.[25]

The circumstances surrounding the purchase of the villa have aroused more than one suspicion. After a tragedy in her family, the heir, the Marchesina Anna Maria Casati Stampa di Soncino, a young woman of 22, decided to sell up at what was widely considered to be an extremely low price: 500 million lire. At the time such a sum was the going price for a good flat in central Milan, but not much more. The Marchesina's legal consultant in the transaction was a bullish young Roman lawyer, Cesare Previti. She allowed the villa's considerable collection of Old Masters and library of antique books to be

---

put it, in a certain sense acknowledged my problem . . . As happens in good families, at a certain moment the father calls the son and resolves the problem'; interrogation published in Veltri and Travaglio, *L'odore dei soldi*, p. 187.

24 Interview with Ferrari, *Il padrone*, p. 65.

25 For a splendid description, Enrico Deaglio, *Besame mucho*, Milan 1995, pp. 135–8. See also Madron, *Le gesta del Cavaliere*, pp. 1–2. Dell'Utri told Madron: 'I find it moving that the affection which Silvio has for his friends extends even to the after-life'; ibid., p. 108.

included in the price. Once the deal was concluded, Previti became Berlusconi's own principal lawyer. He was rapidly to become the third in the troika of leading personalities in the Berlusconi entourage, the other two being Confalonieri and Dell'Utri.[26]

Berlusconi intended to make Arcore his family home. Throughout his twenties he had been, on his own admission, something of a playboy, his lack of height being amply compensated, according to his friend Confalonieri, by his charm and expensive wardrobe.[27] In March 1965, nearly twenty-nine, he married Carla Elvira Dall'Oglio, an elegant but not wealthy girl from La Spezia. They had two children: Maria Elvira (Marina), born in 1966, and Pier Silvio (Dudi), born in 1969. At first the family went to live in a comfortable block of flats in Viale San Gimignano on the periphery of the city. They were joined in the same block by his parents, his aunt Maria Bossi, his cousin Lidia Borsani, and one of his close school friends, Romano Comìncioli. Berlusconi has always wanted to preside over, with generosity and bonhomie, a large group of relatives and friends. This is his 'clan', a word he and his friends use without derogatory significance. The composition of the clan has varied over time, but Berlusconi's instincts have remained the same.

The villa at Arcore needed revamping. In the inimitable style of the nouveau riche, Berlusconi was to introduce a number of novel features. One was an indoor swimming pool with a wall of television

26 *The Economist* investigation of August 2003 (http://www.Economist.com, section 6, 'Your early business career') emphasises in both the Arcore and other transactions the role of the 'enigmatic' figure of Giovanni Dal Santo. Born in Sicily in 1920, by the 1970s Dal Santo was working in Milan as a bookkeeper. He suddenly became the only director of a number of Berlusconi's companies at crucial moments in their shadowy existence, such as Immobiliare Idra when it bought Villa San Martino. According to *The Economist* Dal Santo laundered 2 billion lira (about 5.1 million euros in today's money) through SAF and Coriasco in March 1979.

27 Interview with Ferrari, *Il padrone*, p. 27.

screens at one end of it, presumably to facilitate the new owner's control of his empire while swimming around.[28] After he had secured the villa, Berlusconi contacted Marcello Dell'Utri to offer him the position of factotum with special responsibility for its renovation. Dell'Utri, who after graduating had worked in a series of banks in Palermo, accepted willingly. Sometime after his arrival he brought to Arcore a figure of considerable disrepute. Vittorio Mangano, a young *mafioso* from Palermo, of the powerful family of Porta Nuova, was ostensibly to take charge of the stables, though there was only one horse.

The reasons for Mangano's presence have long been debated and contested. The most plausible is that of the need for protection. In the early 1970s the kidnapping of wealthy entrepreneurs or members of their family was quite widespread in Italy, even in the North. Berlusconi's own family had been threatened in this way. The phenomenon was connected to the fact that a significant number of Mafia bosses had been removed from Sicily, and sent to live under surveillance in the North while they awaited trial. They had used the opportunity to build up their network of criminal contacts throughout Lombardy.[29] It may well be that Dell'Utri installed Mangano as a guarantor for Berlusconi's family. Mangano, however, was not just a bodyguard, let alone a stable boy. Tall, heavily built and taciturn, he was described later by the magistrate Borsellino as 'one of those personalities who acted as a bridgehead for the Mafia organisation in northern Italy.'[30]

Dell'Utri and Berlusconi, though their testimonies vary, have always maintained that once their suspicions were aroused they sent

28 The VIP magazines and approved biographies dwelt lovingly on the other 'optionals' as they chose to call them, using the English word.

29 Corrado Stajano, *La criminalità organizzata in Lombardia*, Milan 1985.

30 See the interview of 1992 published in Veltri and Travaglio, *L'odore dei soldi*, p. 50.

Mangano away from the villa forthwith. Yet Dell'Utri admitted freely that while Mangano was there, there was a great deal of coming and going: 'He sometimes introduced me to these people, saying that they were his friends, but he never mentioned a single name. Names aren't mentioned when people are presented in the Mangano style.'[31] Furthermore, contacts between the two men did not cease. Some years later, in February 1980, Mangano's phone calls from Milan were intercepted by the police for a period of ten days. He made coded phone calls to Palermo and New York. He also spoke, on familiar terms, with Dell'Utri, saying he had business to do with him, as well as 'a horse' – a habitual Mafia way of signifying an undercover deal. Dell'Utri laughed and replied that he did not have 'the small change' for a horse.[32]

Mangano eventually went back to Palermo and became the leader of the Porta Nuova family. He was to be arrested, tried and sentenced to life imprisonment for double homicide, membership of the Mafia and drug trafficking. He died in prison from cancer in 2000, at the age of sixty. Dell'Utri was to become the head of Berlusconi's advertising company, Publitalia, the cash cow of his empire.

31 Ferrari, *Il padrone*, p. 38, and the remarks by the famous anti-Mafia magistrate from Palermo, Giovanni Falcone: 'The Sicilians' tendency to discretion, not to speak of muteness, is proverbial. In the ambit of Cosa Nostra it reaches levels of paroxysm'; *Cose di Cosa Nostra*, Milan 1993, 2nd ed., p. 49.

32 Fiori, *Il venditore*, p. 71, for a detailed account of these interceptions. For an illuminating discussion of Mafia 'horses', D.Gambetta, *The Sicilian Mafia*, Cambridge, Mass. 1993, pp. 18ff.

2: THE MAKING OF A TELEVISION EMPIRE

1. Family crisis

The villa at Arcore was soon ready to receive the Berlusconi family, which took up residence there in the second half of the 1970s. As often happens, extreme luxury offered no guarantee of domestic tranquillity. In 1980, at the age of fourty-four, Berlusconi fell in love with a young, voluptuous and intelligent actress from Bologna, Veronica Lario, twenty years his junior. The *coup de foudre* is said to have occurred at the Teatro Manzoni in Milan, which Berlusconi happened to own, and where Veronica Lario was playing in Fernand Crommelynk's comedy, *Il magnifico cornuto*.[1]

Berlusconi was to fall passionately in love with Lario, but kept his affair hidden for a number of years. He installed Veronica and her mother in one wing of the former Villa Borletti in central Milan – the other wing was his business headquarters – while his family continued to live at Arcore, outside the city. All the testimonies of that time tell of a Berlusconi riven by guilt. His secret love affair

---

1 Fiori, *Il venditore*, pp. 75–76; Mario Oriani (ed.), *Berlusconi story*, Milan 1994, p. 19. Crommelynk's *Le Cocu magnifique* was staged for the first time in Paris in 1920.

conflicted with his loyalty to his family and his deep-felt need to be loved, even worshipped, by all members of his family and entourage. As usual, he tried to reconcile the irreconcilable, and at least in his private life he in part succeeded. When Veronica gave birth to their child, Barbara, in July 1984, he immediately recognised the child, and a year later he and Carla Dall'Oglio separated. It was not to be an acrimonious divorce. Carla was more than adequately provided for, and not banished from the Berlusconi entourage. The two children of the first marriage were to work closely with their father in Fininvest, which in 1984 became the overall name for Berlusconi's group of companies.[2] Marina in particular soon demonstrated many of the business qualities of her father.

Veronica Lario and Silvio Berlusconi were to have two other children – Eleonora and Luigi, born in 1986 and 1988. Theirs was to be a successful as well as unconventional marriage, with Lario playing a role far distant from the stereotypical figure of the uncritical and unconditionally supportive companion of the Great Man. She refused to live at Arcore, sent their children to the Steiner school at Milan, declined to play the First Lady when Berlusconi became Prime Minister, and voiced publicly her disagreement with her husband's support of the Iraq war of 2003. Berlusconi has admitted to loneliness in his time as leader of Italy. His wife has not been by his side, but has made very clear her support and affection for him.[3]

2 Mario Molteni, *Il gruppo Fininvest*, Turin 1997, p. 92.
3 Maria Latella and Veronica Berlusconi, 'Dialogo tra due madri contro la guerra di Bush', *Micromega*, 2003, no. 2, pp. 7–18.

2. Masons

In March 1981 the Milanese magistrates, Gherardo Colombo and Giuliano Turone, while conducting enquiries into the disgraced banker Michele Sindona, came across the list of 962 persons belonging to a secret Masonic lodge, the P2 (Propaganda 2). The list contained a substantial if idiosyncratic section of the nation's power elite. It included the names of all the heads of the secret services, 195 officers of the various armed corps of the Republic, among whom were twelve generals from the Carabinieri, twenty-two from the army, and eight admirals. There were forty-four members of parliament, including three ministers and the secretary of one of the ruling parties, the Social Democrat Pietro Longo. Magistrates, some prefects and heads of police, bankers and businessmen, civil servants and media men made up the remainder of the list. Silvio Berlusconi was on it, at number 1,816 (the numbers went from 1,600 upwards, which suggests that the complete list may never have been found).

The aims of the lodge, whose nominal head, Licio Gelli, seemed too insignificant a figure for the role, were conspiratorial and anti-Communist. The P2 formed part of the secret history which never lay far below the surface of the Italian Republic. Some of that history was farce, some much less so. To reconstruct its subterranean workings is almost impossible. Nearly always the intent was to limit or destroy Italian democracy – though always with the reiterated patriotic goal of saving the country from its principal enemies, the Italian Communist Party (PCI) and the trade unions.

At the time of the lodge's foundation, the PCI had reached the height of its powers, with more than one in three Italians voting for it. To combat its influence, P2 aimed to infiltrate political parties, newspapers and trade unions by means of what one of the organisation's secret documents called 'economic-financial manoeuvres': 'sums not exceeding 30 to 40 billion lira would seem sufficient to allow carefully chosen men, acting in good faith, to conquer key posts necessary for overall control.'[4] In 1977, the lodge had made such progress as to succeed in gaining covert control of Italy's leading newspaper, the *Corriere della Sera*. The fortuitous unmasking of P2 was thus extremely timely. The lodge had devoted itself, in the words of the majority report of the Parliamentary Commission of Inquiry, 'to the pollution of the public life of a nation'.[5]

What was Silvio Berlusconi doing in such an organisation? The most likely answer is 'nothing much', for there is no evidence to show that he played a strategic role within it. He probably joined to extend his range of contacts, to raise his visibility, to continue that extensive 'networking' which his friend Confalonieri rated as one of the keys to his success. Membership could also facilitate the accumulation of capital. During the 1970s, Giovanni Cresti, the director general of Siena's influential bank, the Monte dei Paschi, granted Berlusconi's companies extensive credit on very favourable terms. Although it could not be proved that Cresti was a member of the lodge – his name was not on the list – he was known to be a close friend of Licio Gelli.[6]

4 *Commissione parlamentare d'inchiesta sulla Loggia massonica P2*, vol. 7, pt.1, p. 196. The organisation's two key documents, dating probably from the period 1975–76, entitled 'Memorandum sulla situazione italiana' and 'Piano di rinascita democratica', are published in A.Cecchi, *Storia della P2*, Rome 1985.

5 *Commissione parlamentare d'inchiesta sulla Loggia massonica P2*, Sigla no. 2, *Relazione conclusiva di maggioranza*, p. 164. From 1977 onwards, so it emerged later, the owner of the *Corriere della Sera*, Angelo Rizzoli, was a member of the P2, as were the managing director, Bruno Tassan Din, and the editor, Franco Di Bella. Berlusconi himself wrote a series of articles for the newspaper from 10 April 1978 onwards.

6 See the internal enquiry carried out by the Monte dei Paschi, reported in Fiori, *Il venditore*, pp. 60–3. One hundred and nineteen members of the P2 were employed in banks or in the treasury and finance ministries.

There is no evidence to show that Berlusconi was an active conspirator, but his membership is revealing in a number of ways. One was that he took pains to deny it. In 1988 he was to tell a court in Verona that his membership dated from just before the scandal broke, and that he had never paid an inscription fee. Both statements were untrue. In 1990 the Venetian Court of Appeal condemned him for false testimony. This is the only definitive sentence of guilt that has been passed on him.

The other revealing aspect concerns Berlusconi's political convictions. Even if he was not a leading member of the lodge, he must have been aware of its overall aims. The lodge's anti-Communism, its insistence on the need to destroy the independence of the judiciary and its strategy to take over key elements of the media of that time were all elements that were to figure prominently in Berlusconi's own political project in the future. So, too, was the idea that patriotic values could best be nurtured within a heavily piloted democracy.

3. Commercial television

The 1980s were to witness the transformation of Berlusconi from a highly successful provincial building entrepreneur into a figure of national repute. The vehicle for this transformation was commercial television, then in its infancy in Italy. A number of factors encouraged Berlusconi to make the leap. One was the vulnerability of the Italian building trade, subject to periodic and crippling crises. Another, as he explained on one occasion to Marcello Dell'Utri, was the immediacy that television offered an entrepreneur: 'In the building trade you plan something today and you see it realised in ten years' time. In television you think of it in the morning and in the evening it's already on the screen'. Dell'Utri commented: 'The medium of television was profoundly congenial to Berlusconi's character. It inspired him because of the speed with which he could put into practice the ideas that went through his head. I'd go further: television is Berlusconi.'[7] This symbiotic relationship with the medium of television is fundamental to our understanding of the man.

Another strong motive for his change of direction was that commercial television offered an unprecedented opportunity for him to make quick money. Here, as we shall see below, the role of Berlusconi's advertising company, Publitalia, founded in 1979 and run by Marcello dell'Utri from 1982 onwards, was to be crucial. The increase in its turnover was spectacular: 12 billion lire in 1980; 900 billion by 1984; 2,167 billion by the end of the decade. Already by 1984, 85 percent of Fininvest's income came from the television division, and nearly 2,000 members of its 3,500 workforce were employed there.[8]

Of almost equal significance was the fact that in the early 1980s Berlusconi acquired a political patron of great importance. Bettino Craxi, the leader of the Italian Socialist party, was to become President of the Council of Ministers in 1983. Massive and intimidating, a shrewd tactician and inveterate anti-Communist, Craxi offered a modernising veneer which Italy's two major parties, the Christian Democrats and Communists, both lacked. He, too, was Milanese, very much in tune with the fashion-conscious, high-tech consumerism which characterised the city in the new decade. Under his leadership, politics were to be personalised and simplified, they were to have a strong showbiz element, their principal medium was to be television. There was little that was Socialist in all this, but much of southern

7 Ferrari, *Il padrone*, pp. 69–70.

8 Molteni, *Fininvest*, p. 67, table 4.2; Madron, *Le geste*, p. 102; Sandro Gerbi, 'I conti del Gruppo Berlusconi. Esame del bilancio consolidato 1984', *Problemi dell'Informazione*, vol. 11 (1986), no. 4, pp. 601–8.

European Socialism was going in the same direction in the 1980s. Craxi was to become the ideal guide and protector for Berlusconi. By 1984 the men were firm friends, with Craxi agreeing to be the godfather (*compare*) of Barbara, the child born out of wedlock to Berlusconi and Veronica Lario. No Christian Democrat leader would have considered such a gesture.

Berlusconi viewed his shift into commercial television as something of a crusade, a way of breaking the grip of a staider, more restrictive Italy, which found its cultural expression in the monopoly exercised by RAI, the public broadcasting company. He explained later:

> Viewers avidly desired things that were different from those which the RAI offered . . . they wanted shows that went on late, whereas the RAI closed up shop at 11:00 P.M. Basically, private television was an act of transgression which tempted great numbers of people. I thought about all those things which could enter their homes – game shows, quiz shows, information, but also advertisements and consumer goods.[9]

Here was a ground plan from which he was not to shift for two decades.

~

In France in the early 1980s Bernard Tapie, a figure who resembled Berlusconi in many ways, was reaching the height of his popularity. Tapie offered the French the three 'Rs': '*le Rêve, le Rire, le Risque*'. He claimed these to be a rule of life far superior to that which the Agnelli family had evolved for FIAT and for the Juventus football team. There, in Turin, the three 'Ss' reigned supreme: '*Semplicità, Serietà, Sobrietà*'.

---

9 Ferrari, *Il padrone*, p. 70.

Tapie and Berlusconi, as well as Murdoch in the earlier part of his career, all wanted to contest and break free from the old elites, both in business and in public institutions.[10] Tapie made his first fortune by buying up old and ailing firms, restructuring and downsizing them ferociously, and then selling them off again. He rapidly became a business idol in France. In April 1985, at the Grand Auditorium of the Palais des Congrès in Paris, he staged what was described as France's first 'business show'. Invited by the École Supérieure des Dirigeants d'Entreprise (ESDE), he filled the auditorium (capacity of 4,000) twice over. Hundreds of young people came to hear him. The journalist Anne Sinclair asked him: 'How did you get to where you are?' Tapie replied: 'Because I love myself', a reply that Berlusconi would very much have appreciated. In early 1986 Tapie launched his television programme *Ambitions*. Young people were given the chance to start their own businesses, and the programme followed their progress. *Ambitions*, which was transmitted at 8:30 P.M. on Friday evening, gained an initial audience share of 34 percent.[11]

Tapie's success was in many ways more spectacular than that of Berlusconi – he was a more accomplished showman – but the Italian's was more soundly based. Tapie compèred programmes on television, Berlusconi bought up the television stations themselves. Structural conditions in Italy were on his side. Throughout the 1980s, a decade which has rightly been described as fatal for the sector, Italian commercial television was left without regulation.[12] Back in July 1976, the

10 Murdoch was incensed in particular by British complacency and snobbishness. 'They distrust money,' he asserted. 'They despise business. They create the social and psychological currents which have done so much damage to Britain and its willingness to change'; Shawcross, *Murdoch*, p. 31, as well as Bouchet, *Tapie*, p. 26.

11 J. Villeneuve, *Le mythe Tapie*, Paris 1988, pp. 52–7 and 64–7.

12 Paolo Caretti, 'Informazione: l'anomalia italiana', *Democrazia e Diritto*, vol. 41 (2003), no. 1, pp. 169–70. The Constitutional Court was to intervene frequently on these issues, but without conspicuous success.

Italian Constitutional Court had laid down some guidelines. National broadcasting was to be reserved for public television, but local commercial operators could henceforth begin transmissions.[13] The Court declared that ether was a collective resource and asked parliament to legislate with urgency for the whole area of the mass media. In particular, it requested respect for what it called internal and external pluralism. The first was to ensure that the different voices of Italian civil society found expression on television. The second that the ownership of television channels should not be unduly concentrated.

All this was wilfully ignored by the politicians of the time, and by Bettino Craxi in particular. At just 11.4 percent of the electorate in 1983, the Italian Socialists were still far too small a force for the ambitions of their leader. Craxi had the power of veto over the formation of government coalitions, he could even become President of the Council of Ministers, but he wanted the Socialists to be a great European force, like their Spanish or French counterparts. The unhindered and meteoric rise of his friend Berlusconi was a unique opportunity for increasing the media influence and clientelistic networks of his own party.[14]

The result was that years passed during which an unchecked free-for-all reigned in the world of commercial television. These were perfect conditions for Silvio Berlusconi. He was the most dynamic of the new television entrepreneurs, the one who was prepared to sail

13 Local commercial transmissions were to be permitted on the grounds that there were sufficient frequencies available 'to permit the freedom of private initiative without danger of private monopolies or oligopolies'; A.Pace, 'La radiotelevisone in Italia con particolare riguardo alla emittenza privata,'*Rivista Trimestrale di Diritto Pubblico*, vol. 37 (1987) no. 3, p. 623.

14 The Italian journalist Piero Ottone recounted in 1994: 'I have followed his [Craxi's] activities over the years, on occasion at close quarters, and I remember the superhuman efforts he made to prevent Parliament from passing legislation on television regulation'; 'L'Italia dei furbi', *Ulisse*, vol. 7 (1994), no. 12; quoted in Fiori, *Il venditore*, p. 100.

closest to the wind in legal terms, and who seemed to have access to the greatest quantities of capital. His principal competition at the time, Edilio Rusconi of the Rusconi publishing group, who owned the channel Rete 4, and Mario Formenton of the Mondadori group, which owned Italia 1, were both convinced that antitrust legislation was on its way, and that they could not stray too far from local transmission. Only Berlusconi risked illegality, buying up local stations in the whole of the peninsula, ensuring clear reception, and explicitly establishing a national network for his Canale 5, the heir of the little TeleMilano of Milano 2. Naturally enough, he was opposed to any regulation, for here was negative freedom at work in undiluted form.[15] By 1984 he had bought out both Rusconi and Formenton. With his three major channels, Canale 5, Rete 4 and Italia 1, transmitting nationally, he had established a near monopoly.

On 16 October 1984, three magistrates from Turin, Rome and Pescara respectively gave orders for Berlusconi's television stations to be partially blacked out. Their argument was very simple. The ruling of the Constitutional Court in 1976 made provision for *local* but not *national* commercial broadcasting, and Berlusconi's three national channels were in breach of these provisions. A significant part of Italy found itself without Mediaset transmissions. It was a disconcerting experience. That day its programmes included the favourite childrens' cartoon, *The Smurfs*, *Dallas, Dynasty* and *High Noon* (all scheduled for Canale 5), as well as *New York, New York* on Rete 4. It was not a good moment to have a blank screen.[16]

---

15 He told Alberto Statera in 1983: 'For my part, I am convinced that there is no need for any legislation, because the market, here as elsewhere, contains all the antibodies necessary to regulate itself'; A.Statera, 'Silvio Berlusconi', in N.Ajello et al., *Perché loro*, Bari 1984, p. 217.

16 The best reconstruction of this extraordinary event and its aftermath is to be found in Fiori, *Il venditore*, pp. 105–20, upon which my own account is heavily dependent.

Predictably enough, the popular outcry was considerable. Berlusconi's channels, which continued to transmit to the rest of the country, fanned the flames, demanding respect for a new citizen's right, 'freedom to use the television's automatic controls' (*libertà di telecomando*). In the face of this mediatic crisis, the first in the history of the Italian Republic, Bettino Craxi reacted with a speed and determination which could only have been called exemplary had they been employed for another and worthier cause. The Council of Ministers was summoned to meet on Saturday, 20 October, and immediately issued a decree law (*decreto legge*), valid for six months, ordering the resumption of national commercial transmissions. At the same time the new Socialist spokesman for telecommunications, Paolo Pillitteri, Craxi's brother-in-law and later to be mayor of Milan, announced: 'The magistrates' initiative is all the more inappropriate at a moment when parliament is in the process of examining and refining a new law on private television transmissions.'[17] In the event, the law regulating telecommunications was only passed in August 1990, fourteen years after the Constitutional Court had invoked its necessity. The new law merely sanctioned the status quo, leaving Berlusconi's empire untouched.

~

This unedifying story was dense with implications. All over the world the relationship between media ownership and political power has been an intimate one. After Rupert Murdoch threw the weight of his newspapers (*The Sun* and *The News of the World*) behind Mrs. Thatcher in the 1979 elections, she wrote to thank *The Sun*'s editor Larry Lamb, and in 1980 knighted him for his 'services to journalism'. When Murdoch took over *The Times* and *The Sunday Times* in 1981,

17 Ibid., p. 109.

his bid was not referred to the Monopolies Commission. The pledges he gave on editorial independence were soon to be flouted, but no action was taken against him. Throughout the 1980s, Thatcher and Murdoch were linked in a close relationship, two faces of the same relentless neoliberal drive towards deregulation and the concentration of power. Murdoch came to control British satellite television and 36 percent of its printed press.[18]

There are many other such stories. Israel Asper, for instance, became Canada's senior media tycoon in the year 2000 when he bought up most of Conrad Black's Canadian media holdings. Asper worked closely with Canada's current Prime Minister, Jean Chrétien, and as a result strongly discouraged criticism of him in any part of his Can West Global Communications. In France in the 1980s, Robert Hersant, the right-wing owner of a very considerable media empire, courted assiduously both Jacques Chirac and Valéry Giscard d'Estaing. One of Giscard's closest lieutenants even held a post at the Socpresse, Hersant's major holding company.[19]

The Italian case went still further because it involved the regulation, or rather the lack of it, of the *entire* commercial television sector. In the 1970s, the Italian political class had already effectively divided public television between them, with RAI 1 a fiefdom of the Christian Democrats, RAI 2 of the Socialists, and RAI 3 of the Communists. This could hardly be considered correct practice, or the encouragement of a tradition of public broadcasting autonomy, but at least there existed a plurality of voices and positions.[20] No such pluralism, either

18 Eldridge, Kitzinger and Williams, *Mass Media*, pp. 33–42; Shawcross, *Murdoch*, p. 210.

19 For Hersant, see Tunstall and Palmer, *Media Moguls*, pp. 141–51; for Asper, see Cathryn Atkinson's obituary, *Guardian*, 16 October 2003.

20 For a detailed and convincing history of the RAI, see Franco Monteleone, *Storia della radio e della televisione in Italia*, 3rd ed., Venice 2003. RAI television had begun in 1954.

internal or external, was to reign for the private sector. In the 1980s, Bettino Craxi, much more so than the Christian Democrats, realised how rich were the pickings to be had there, and how formidable an operator was his friend from Milan.[21] His were valid enough considerations from a narrowly party point of view, but they were poison for Italian democracy in the key area of media policy.

4. 'Non è la RAI'

The commercial television system which Berlusconi built up was profoundly American in character, and was to have a conspicuous effect upon the cultural life of the nation. It is worth describing in detail. Berlusconi organised the programming of his channels substantially as a mixture of films and telefilms, quiz and variety shows, cartoons and sport, with football preeminent in this last category. He operated under one peculiar restriction. Until the telecommunications law of August 1990, Italian commercial television was prohibited from broadcasting live. The most important consequence of this prohibition, which was all the stranger for being maintained in a context otherwise dominated by total *laissez-faire*, was the impossibility of presenting news bulletins.

For the rest, Berlusconi rapidly acquired a vast library of old films, telefilms and cartoons, buying up liberally from the archives of Titanus in particular, but also MGM, Warner, Disney and some American television companies. Carlo Freccero made good use of the films for one of the earliest and most successful programmes of Canale 5, *Pomeriggio con sentimento* (1981), which showed a classic American or

21 A convincing analysis of the relationships that developed in and around the Socialist party in the 1980s is to be found in Luciano Cafagna, *Una strana disfatta*, Venice 1996, esp. pp. 138–9.

Italian film every afternoon from 2:00 P.M. onwards, and which set the tone for afternoon programming on Italian television. What was true of the afternoon was also true of the morning. *Buongiorno Italia* (Canale 5, 1981), modelled on *Good Morning America*, with its cooking tips, women's fashion, gymnastic exercises and so on, introduced the Italians, especially housewives, to the delights of breakfast television. Quiz shows were primarily in the safe hands of Italy's veteran compère, Mike Bongiorno, an iconic figure who had been responsible for the nation's most famous quiz show, *Lascia o raddoppia?*, which dated back to 1955.[22] Berlusconi had recruited him from the RAI at a very early date, and his *I sogni nel cassetto* marked the official opening of Canale 5 in November 1980.[23] The working friendship between the two men has lasted more than two decades. As for telefilms and soap operas, they were once again American, and only later in small part Brazilian and Italian. In 1982 Canale 5's *Flamingo Road* and *Dallas* vied with Retequattro's *Dynasty*; in 1983 its mini-series *Thornbirds*, bought from the ABC, was triumphant over Retequattro's very costly *Winds of War* (Paramount and ABC). Cartoons were at first American and then increasingly Japanese. *The Simpsons* arrived on Canale 5 in 1991. Finally, football was first represented by *Mundialito* (Canale 5, 1982), a competition between club sides of different nations, which had originated in Uruguay but which Canale 5 was to make its own in the 1980s.[24]

---

22 See the seminal article by Umberto Eco, 'Verso una civiltà della visione?' (1961), now published as 'Fenomenologia di Mike Bongiorno' in his *Diario minimo*, Milan 1992, pp. 29–34.

23 The party to launch the new quiz show, which offered prizes far superior to those of the RAI, took place on the banks of the artificial lake at the centre of Milano 2; Molteni, *Fininvest*, p. 71.

24 The encyclopaedic and indispensable guide to the history of Italian television programmes is Aldo Grasso, *Storia della televisione italiana*, 2nd ed., Milan 2000. The dates in brackets in my text refer to the year in which programmes were first screened.

In terms of content, it is important to stress that Berlusconi's massive importation of American material was to a great extent indiscriminate, in the sense of not being subject on his part to rigorous ideological censorship. What mattered was audience levels, not political correctness. Hollywood films were transmitted which sometimes expressed values far distant from Berlusconi's own. Cartoons like *The Smurfs*, with their ecological emphasis, or *The Simpsons*, which highlights losers rather than winners in American life, could in no way be considered 'organic' to Berlusconi's project.[25] At this early stage popularity was all.

One of the few areas of distinction, in Bourdieu's sense of the term, came with variety shows, omnipresent on Italian television. Here not only was production autochthonous, but the styling of some of Berlusconi's programmes was significantly innovative. *Drive in* (Italia 1, 1983) was paradigmatic in this respect. Its mixture of demented humour, repetitiveness, imitations, even transgression – with early barbs against rampant Milanese yuppies – its fragmented and chaotic timing, invented television slang and scarcely clad vallettes marked it off stridently from the staider RAI productions of the time. *Drive in*, which from 1984 went on the air on Sundays at 8:30 P.M., and which was repeated until 1988, enjoyed a mass youth following.[26] In broad terms, Berlusconi's three channels were designed for different audiences: Italia 1 was aimed at youth, Retequattro catered primarily to housewives and pensioners, and Canale 5 was designated for family viewing.

The gender politics of this new commercial television are fascinating, but very rarely touched upon. Let us look at the body first. Berlusconi is often held responsible for enticing Italian housewives to undress in front of the television cameras, but this is not strictly true,

25 On *The Simpsons*, Paul Cantor's excellent 'The Simpsons: atomist politics and the nuclear family', *Political Theory*, vol. 27 (1999), no. 6, pp. 734–49.

26 Grasso, *Storia della televisione italiana*, pp. 400–2.

nor part of his style. Umberto Smaila's programme, *Colpo grosso* (Italia 7, 1987), a show which involved young Italians of both sexes gaining quiz points by slowly shedding their clothing (though never their underpants), was not broadcast on one of Berlusconi's channels.[27] Nor was its formula copied by them. On the other hand, Mediaset's programmes *were* heavily sexually oriented, in a lecherous way that stopped just short of nudity. Every middle-aged compère was, and still is, accompanied by scantily dressed soubrettes. Cameras zoomed in upon them from below and behind, emphasizing anatomical detail whenever possible. Rarely had the 'erotic gaze' been so crudely constructed.[28] This was a very far cry from the RAI. So, too, was the explicitly titled 'Non è la Rai' (Canale 5, 1991), broadcast at lunchtime, with its numerous cast of very young girls dancing provocatively in body stockings to the popular music of the time. To be one of them was the dream of every thirteen-year-old Italian girl returning from school, to desire them the fate of every man who had ever read Nabokov's *Lolita*.

Beyond body politics and the representations of desire lay more general gender choices. Women, not only on Mediaset but on the RAI as well, were almost always treated as decorative 'chickens' (*galline*), without an idea in their heads. They could aspire to be newscasters. In exceptional cases, like Raffaella Carrà, they could run their own variety shows. But there was no inkling of gender equality, no influence, however slight, of the feminism of those years. Quite the contrary. Avuncular condescension reigned supreme, ripe with sexual innuendo, though sometimes masked by an old-style gallantry. Women were required to play along, and did.

27 However, it is true that Berlusconi indirectly controlled, by means of Publitalia, the publicity revenues and thus the lifeblood of Italia 7.

28 See the renowned article by Laura Mulvey, 'Visual Pleasure and Narrative Cinema', *Screen*, vol. 16 (1975), no. 3, and the ensuing debate.

When analysing a media culture, its silences are as important as its noises. On Berlusconi's channels there was a lot of entertainment but little room for the real world. The ban on live broadcasting certainly did not help, but what documentaries there were tended to be on animals, not humans, with the result that it was easier to be informed about the habitat of penguins than social conditions in southern Italy. In general, Mediaset made few programmes itself. Although it enjoyed the luxury of broadcasting on three national channels, it made no space for a quality arm of commercial television, such as that constituted by the British Channel 4 from 1982 onwards. Such an omission was to cost, and still costs, Berlusconi dear in terms of his overall cultural image.

4. The publicity empire

Advertising revenue was the driving force and determinant of Berlusconi's television, with audience ratings the undisputed arbiter of programme choices. As Nora Rizzi has explained, the aim of commercial television in general was *not* 'to know how to produce programmes, which is or should be the rule in public television, but to know how to produce, by means of the programmes on offer, television audiences; that is, the consumers required by the market of investors in publicity.'[29]

In this exercise, Berlusconi proved to be a master. Conditions were extremely favourable for him. By the 1980s in Italy there were several thousand firms which wished to advertise more fully on television but were unable to do so. The tradition of advertising on

29 Nora Rizza, 'Il palinsesto come fattore di produzione. Evoluzione delle logiche di programmazione nell'emittenza commerciale', *Problemi dell'Informazione*, vol. 15 (1990), no. 4, p. 530.

Italian public television had been a carefully restricted one. It was in line with the policy of most European public television, and derived in particular from the early Christian Democrats' diffidence towards unregulated consumer culture. From 1957 onwards, publicity on the RAI had been concentrated principally in the legendary *Carosello*. Broadcast at 8:50 P.M. for ten minutes, after the news and before the children went to bed, *Carosello* featured four or five little stories, at the end of each of which the product being advertised was briefly nominated.[30]

As always with the Christian Democrats, behind noble intentions lay more squalid realities. The RAI's associated advertising company, Sipra, under the control of the redoubtable Colonel Fiore, granted the limited advertising space available as if performing a personal, political and religious dispensation. The breaking of this clientelistic monopoly offered great opportunities.[31]

Berlusconi made the most of his chances. His rivals in early commercial television, Rusconi and Mondadori, were both major owners of print media, with considerable experience selling advertising space to firms. Berlusconi soon outdid them both. His boast, behind which lay considerable acumen, was: 'I don't sell space, I sell sales.'[32] In other words, he wished to guarantee to potential advertisers not just the insertion of a certain number of spots at fixed times, but the control of the whole environment in which the advertisement was located, ensuring value for money and above all increased sales of the product in question. Television advertising derives its being from a golden chain of connection: from the marketing department of a firm to the advertising agency, to the crew making the spot, to the television company and its programmes, finally to the consumer

30 O. Calabrese, *Carosello o dell'educazione serale*, Florence 1975.
31 D'Anna and Moncalvo (eds), *Berlusconi in Concert*, pp. 63–4.
32 Fiori, *Il venditore*, p. 93.

at home. Berlusconi tried to intervene in as many parts of this process as he could. In particular, he cut out the advertising agencies, offering instead a direct line to his television channels, with Publitalia absorbing the 15 percent fee charged by the agencies.[33]

In his new crusade, Berlusconi mobilised both himself and Publitalia's army of young salesmen. Important customers were invited individually to Arcore, charmed over lunch, and promised special discounts and efficient follow-up services. Some were even treated to Berlusconi at the piano. It was a far cry from the queue outside colonel Fiore's office at Sipra. Berlusconi issued precise instructions to his team of salesmen. They were, like him, to have the 'sun in their pockets', to exude optimism and courtesy. They were forbidden to smoke or have long hair, or beards, or even moustaches. Their breath was to be fresh and their hair without dandruff. They were never to put their briefcases on the table of their client, nor take off their jackets in his presence. They had to memorise the birthdays of their clients, as well as those of their wives and children. Flowers for their secretaries, mimosa on women's day (8 March). Above all, no sweaty handshakes. In his 'Confidential advice for selling advertising space', an informal lecture of 1994, Berlusconi said, 'On the basis of my professional experience, I can confide to you that I have always won by being professional. If I've always won out, it's been rarely thanks to my talent, a few times thanks to the luck of an amateur, but I have always won thanks to technique.'[34] As early as 1983, Publitalia had cornered 43 percent of the total market of television advertising.[35]

Publitalia was never to relax its grip in the coming years. In 1995 Marialina Marcucci, the owner of Videomusic, a small, independent commercial channel with a strong youth audience, recounted how she

33 Molteni, *Il gruppo Fininvest*, p. 74.
34 D'Anna and Moncalvo (eds), *Berlusconi in Concert*, p. 300.
35 Gerbi, 'I conti del gruppo Berlusconi', p. 601.

had been forced to sell up. By hogging the whole market in television publicity, Publitalia had made it impossible for small companies like hers to survive:

> I remember once, it was at the end of the eighties, that we had signed an agreement with [the ice cream company] Algida for their summer campaign of advertisements. It was a contract worth 70 million lira in all: peanuts compared with the sort of sums that were being spent on advertising on Silvio Berlusconi's channels. Even so, the Publitalia sellers of advertising space tried to undercut us. They offered Algida very favourable terms if the company agreed to spend all its advertising budget on the Fininvest channels. . . . All in all, you could say that the only company that has never let itself be intimidated by Publitalia has been Coca-Cola. . . . Usually, though, the firms give way. And from their point of view it's quite comprehensible because they have their budgets to balance.[36]

According to David Forgacs' calculations, in 1984 the RAI showed 46,080 advertisements for a total of 311 hours of advertising, whereas commercial channels showed 494,000 advertisements for a total of 3,468 hours; in all, circa 1,500 television advertisements per day were being shown in Italy, more than in all the other European countries put together.[37] The onslaught was not only temporal but aural: volume automatically increased at advertisement time, not only for adults' programmes but children's as well. There was little in all this of Vance Packard's famous 'hidden persuaders'.[38] Italian commer-

36 C.Gallucci, 'Sola contro un dannato Biscione', *L'Espresso*, vol. 41 (1995), no. 11, 17 March, pp. 47–50.

37 D.Forgacs, *Italian Culture in the Industrial Era, 1880–1980*, Manchester 1990, pp. 184–5.

38 Vance Packard, *Hidden Persuaders*, New York 1957.

cial television advertisements in the 1980s were a noisy, endlessly repetitive, frontal attack upon fledgling consumers as well as hardened veterans of the world of goods.[39] Children's programmes were constantly interrupted as Gig toys, one of the leaders in the sector, displayed with blaring tones the full range of its robots, castles and racing cars for the boys, and dolls, their houses and their clothes for the girls. No one should underestimate the effect of such a barrage in forming, and not just reflecting, family patterns of consumption.

Far from separating out programmes, film stories and advertisers' names, as in *Carosello*, Berlusconi's channels strove to create a seamless web between programmes and adverts. In this they followed a consolidated American tradition, which had begun with *The Maxwell House Showboat*, a radio programme of the 1930s, and had flowered in the golden age of American television in the 1950s, with programmes like the *Kraft Television Theater*.[40] Mike Bongiorno, once again, was the innovator in Italy. In *Superflash*, a 1982 quiz show, he adopted the American habit of himself sponsoring a product in the heart of the transmission. Others followed suit. Suddenly compères were sipping coffee in the middle of their shows, eating salami and smacking their lips, lying down on mattresses, carefully aided by the ever-attendant soubrettes. Some of the more intelligent TV compères adopted a vaguely ironical approach, others simply went through a dull and servile routine in return for a great deal of money.

~

How far was this different in any way from the other commercial televisions which were flourishing all over the world at the same

---

39 For an interesting analysis of the type and quantity of advertisements in these years, R. Grandi, *Come parla la pubblicità*, Milan 1987, especially p. 14.

40 Greg Myers, *Ad Worlds*, London 1999, p. 117.

time? Certainly, there was a great deal that was quintessentially American – not just the programmes themselves, but the quantity of advertising and the overall style. However, certain key elements distinguish the Italian experience from others. First, in no other democracy did commercial television develop under the almost complete control of a single individual. Second, no regulatory body was set up to oversee standards. The Guarantor for Telecommunications, introduced in 1990, was designed to be toothless from birth. Third, Italian public television lacked the traditions to respond to the new challenge of commercial competitors in a way that would distinguish it from its challenger. Too dependent upon the political parties and lacking an autonomous culture, the RAI ended up by aping Mediaset and competing with it exclusively on its own terms – those of audience rating. Only RAI 3 constituted a partial exception. Overall, though, there was no public television to fly the flag of editorially independent news, civic responsibility, well-researched documentaries and quality programmes which could appeal at different times to both majorities and special interests. The Italian viewing public was profoundly bereft of all of this.

Of course, the debate about the degree to which media, and television in particular, determine people's culture and eventually their political allegiance is a wide-ranging and complicated one. Certainly, it would be foolish to assume that individuals and families simply imbibed the oft-repeated messages of the new commercial television. In the Italian case, at least one study has revealed how delicate the connections are between viewing and family values, and how much translation, criticism and rejection is involved in the reception of television programmes.[41] However, it would be even more foolhardy to claim that the influence of television is marginal.

41 F.Casetti (ed.), *L'ospite fisso*, Milano 1995.

In Italy, the Eurisko survey of 1986 compared the frequency of certain key elements of cultural consumption: 86.3 percent of interviewees watched television on a daily basis, compared to only 46.4 percent who listened to the radio and 41.4 percent who read a newspaper. Only 17 percent went to the cinema once or more a month, and 6.1 percent to a museum. Television was the only daily 'cultural' activity of the average Italian family.[42]

In the same year of the Eurisko survey, the novelist Alberto Moravia recounted in a delicate article in the *Corriere della Sera* his experience of being seen on television, and reflected on what exactly television was:

> Those who [have seen me on television] greet me in the street with sincere affection. . . . But when I ask them if they have read any of my work they often reply, without much apparent regret, that because they go to work they have no time to read. And here we come to the mystery of what television really is, of whether it is a pastime or something else. The reply that they give me signifies implicitly that, since they find time for television, but not for reading, then the mass media in question is not a traditional pastime. So what is it then? This is the point I wanted to get to. Television, I think, is something like sleeping or eating: a physiological need, which reading obviously isn't. In any case, the record for the disassociation that television produces between me as pure image and me as a writer came some days ago in Verona. In the main square of the city, a girl came running up to me

42 G.Calvi (ed.), *Indagine sociale italiana. Rapporto 1986*, Milan 1986, p. 172 and table 5.14, p. 173. For a good introduction to the way in which the vast debate on the influence of the media has developed over time, see J.Curren, M.Gurrevitch and J.Woollacott, 'The study of the media: theoretical approaches', in O. Boyd-Barrett and P.Braham (eds), *Media, Knowledge and Power*, London 1987, pp. 57–79. On television and the family, see the important works of David Morley, *Family Television: Cultural Power and Domestic Leisure*, London 1986, and *Home Territories, Media, Mobility and Identity*, London 2000.

and exclaimed: 'How happy I am to make your acquaintance: who are you?' The phrase signified that she had already seen me on television, and as a result she loved me; but she had no idea who I was.[43]

Given the nature of television as a particular 'physiological need,' and the subtle powers of 'pure image', it might have been expected that the advent in Italy of its commercial version would give rise to prolonged debate. The opposite was the case. Instead, a grotesque duopoly was created: on the one side a flagging public broadcasting system, on the other the suffocating preeminence of Berlusconi's three channels. The combination produced a deeply conformist, repetitive and uncritically consumer-oriented television system pumped out not just from 2001, when Berlusconi won political power in a decisive fashion, but from the early 1980s onwards. The connection between this twenty-year period of cultural conditioning and Berlusconi's eventual political triumph is a fundamental one. I shall return to it in the second part of this book, when analysing Berlusconi's overall political project.

~

It is worth adding a word on Berlusconi's other media property, especially his print interests. As I wrote at the beginning of this book, Berlusconi has distinguished himself for being a television tycoon rather than a newspaper baron. Television has been the medium that he has most understood, loved and exploited. Nonetheless, he also built up a considerable print empire. At its heart was *Sorrisi e Canzoni*, a typical television-oriented weekly magazine which combines the

---

43 Alberto Moravia, 'Amare il prossimo di affetto televisivo,' *Corriere della Sera*, 20 August 1986; quoted in Aldo Grasso, *Storia della televisione italiana*, pp. 455–6.

times of the programmes with information and gossip about them. Berlusconi was careful not to exclude the stars and starlets of the RAI, and to offer accurate information on the schedules of all the Italian television channels. He was rewarded with a circulation of some three million copies by November 1986. He also invested in the newspaper *Il Giornale*, which had as its editor the veteran journalist Indro Montanelli. This story, though, did not end well, because Montanelli became increasingly exasperated by the owner's interference in the editorial line of the paper, and eventually left along with much of his staff. Montanelli, a liberal conservative, was then to become one of Berlusconi's most implacable critics until his death in July 2001, at the age of ninety-two. *Il Giornale* is presently owned by Berlusconi's brother, Paolo, but has never flowered into being Italy's major conservative newspaper. That title still belongs firmly to the *Corriere della Sera*, which sells 685,000 copies per day, compared to the 220,000 of *Il Giornale*.

Last but not least, in 1990 Italy's largest publishing house, Mondadori, became part of Berlusconi's empire. The battle for its control proved to be a very bitter one. It was resolved only by a Roman court of law, which found in favour of Berlusconi and against his rival Carlo De Benedetti, at the time the owner of Olivetti. However, in 2003, Cesare Previti, the lawyer who had joined the Berlusconi clan after the purchase of Arcore, was condemned to eleven years' imprisonment for having successfully corrupted the Roman judges in the original court case. Only the Italian legal system, which allows a defendant to go free until condemned by all three grades of justice, kept Previti out of prison.[44]

44 See ch. 6 below, p. 145.

5. Football

Since childhood, Berlusconi had been an ardent fan of the famous Milanese football club, AC Milan. His father had taken him regularly to the stadium on Sundays. In March 1986, as the crowning element of what was an outstandingly successful decade, Berlusconi decided to buy up the ailing club. It belonged, so he said, to 'the sphere of affections', not to that of economic calculation.[45] He hesitated a long time before making the purchase. He was afraid of being seen as too narrowly partisan by a nation renowned for its divided loyalties, both on and off the field. But in 1982 Italy had won its first World Cup since the Fascist period, and national football fever was then at its height. The opportunity to link personal and municipal sporting triumph to national television audiences and both to consumer advertising was too great for Berlusconi to turn down. In July 1986, the members of the new AC Milan team were presented to 10,000 fans at the city's Arena. The team arrived by helicopter, with loudspeakers playing Wagner's *The Ride of the Walkyries*: 'I knew very well that people would laugh at me,' Berlusconi recounted later, 'even treat me with irony. But we needed to show that the whole way of thinking at AC Milan had changed.'[46] The event was subsequently transmitted repeatedly on all three of his television channels. For the new 1986–87 season some 65,000 season tickets were sold, an all-time record.

In France, 1986 was also the year in which Bernard Tapie bought up the Olympique of Marseilles, another ailing football team, though much less famous than Berlusconi's AC Milan. Both men were rapidly to take their clubs to a series of unexpected national and international

45 Ferrari, *Il padrone*, p. 129.
46 Ibid., pp. 134–5.

triumphs – sure proof, or so it seemed, that their business dynamism could be successfully applied to other fields. Tapie, indeed, was to be first into the political arena, using his new-found popularity at Marseilles to launch his career first as a Socialist then as a Radical politician. His triumphs, though, were short-lived. Embroiled in a number of financial scandals, in 1996–97 he fell rapidly from grace and was eventually condemned by the courts.[47]

Berlusconi has lasted the course very much better. At AC Milan, as elsewhere in his business empire in the early part of his career, there was significant evidence of bold and unconventional choices which paid off handsomely. Just as Hollywood films, if they were popular enough, were to be shown on television regardless of their content, so Milan was to acquire new players, and a new manager, who were far from conformist. The élan of Dutch football of the time came to light up the grey Sunday afternoons at the San Siro stadium. Marc Van Basten, Ruud Gullit and Frank Rijkaard were at the heart of the new team, alongside outstanding Italian defenders like Franco Baresi and the young Paolo Maldini. Gullit was a special case. His family came from Suriname, he wore dreadlocks in the manner of Bob Marley, and was committed to antiracism at an international level. His speed and elegance on the field entranced the Milanese fans. Within a few months San Siro's terraces were full of youths with their faces painted black, their hair coloured with the red and black of Milan AC, and with dreadlocks falling over their shoulders. Berlusconi, too, espoused an antiracist position: 'I explained to them [the fan clubs] that it was possible to support a club without being violent or intolerant. The Milanese fans that I had inherited were those who unfurled banners with anti-Semitic and racist slogans on them. That mentality had to go.'[48]

---

47 Bouchet, *Tapie*, pp. 39ff; André Bercoff, *Comment ils ont tué Tapie*, Paris 1998.
48 Ferrari, *Il padrone*, p. 135.

In 1987 the little-known Arrigo Sacchi arrived as Milan's new manager. His combination of constant pressing, marking by zone and almost mathematical organisation of the relationship between defence, midfield and attack, was highly controversial but bore almost immediate fruit in the hothouse atmosphere of the new AC Milan. The team won the Italian championship in 1988. At Barcellona in May 1989 it crushed Steana Bucharest 4–0 to take the European Champion's Cup.[49] At the end of the same year it won the Intercontinental Cup, the highest possible accolade for a club team. AC Milan's successes were to continue throughout the early 1990s.

As has often been pointed out, football metaphors abound in Berlusconi's language, and the name of his political party, Forza Italia ('go for it, Italy!') derives from the chanting of the fans of Italy's national team. Soccer was Italy's 'deep play'.[50] It was an abiding passion, revelatory of elements of the nation's deeper popular culture of which Berlusconi aspired to be the foremost interpreter. In the 1980s in Italy the game was big business, as it was to become in Britain ten years later. Football fed naturally into television and played to huge audiences, passive recipients of ever-greater amounts of advertising. Postgame analyses took up peak viewing time on many channels on Sunday and Monday night, reaching grotesque levels of repetition. The links between global markets, television advertising and club ownership were visible everywhere.

By the end of the 1980s Berlusconi had achieved everything he could have wished for. Of course, as with all tycoons worth the

49 In order to transport 26,000 fans to Barcellona, the club chartered a ship, twenty-five aeroplanes and 450 buses.

50 Clifford Geertz, *The Interpretation of Cultures*, New York 1973, pp. 448–51. Cockfighting in Bali, the object of his study, is 'set aside from [everyday] life as "only a game" and reconnected to it as "more than a game"' (ibid., p. 450). For an extended discussion of football as Italy's 'deep play', see P. Ginsborg, *Italy and its Discontents*, London 2001, pp. 112–19.

name, there was no question of stopping there. 'Let's be sincere,' he said in 1989, when a journalist asked him if he would consider selling AC Milan now that he had transformed it so successfully, 'in the whole of my life I have never bought anything, however small, with the slightest intention of it being sold again.'[51] Patrimonial instincts such as these were unusual. So too, as we shall see, was Berlusconi's determination to defend what he had acquired.

51 Ferrari, *Il padrone*, p. 136. On Berlusconi and football, see also the interesting chapter in Tobias Jones, *The Dark Heart of Italy*, London 2003, pp. 61–85.

3: INTO POLITICS

1. Clean hands

It can safely be said, paradoxical though it may appear, that without the reforming zeal of Francesco Saverio Borrelli, the distinguished magistrate who was to become the Chief Procurator at Milan, Silvio Berlusconi would never have been Italy's Prime Minister. By the beginning of the 1990s, Berlusconi had every reason to be content with his lot. Not only was he Italy's outstanding businessman, but he was protected, even cosseted, by the ruling group of Italy's politicians. In 1989 the so-called 'CAF' had come into being. Its name derived from the first letters of the surnames of the three men who had created it, the Socialist Bettino Craxi, the Christian Democrats Giulio Andreotti and Arnaldo Forlani. It was they who piloted through parliament the Telecommunications' Law of 1990, so favourable to Berlusconi's new empire.

The 'normal' relationship in a neoliberal democracy between media tycoon and sympathetic political leadership was thus in full swing. Each has its own sphere of operations. The media tycoon lurks *behind* politics, but is not *in* politics. He derives advantage from the actions of sympathetic politicians, and repays it with conspicuous and benevolent treatment of the same. There is a whole history to be written of the regulatory and legislative favours granted in modern democracies on these bases.[1] Italy was no exception. The Act of 1990 not only confirmed Berlusconi's near monopoly of commercial televsion. It also allowed him to transmit 'live', and thus to compete with the RAI in its last area of prerogative: the making of the news. Personal tensions and factional rivalries obviously remained, but the ground had been laid in Italy for a serene, pernicious and long-term cohabitation between television power on the one hand and politics on the other.

Instead, all this was swept away by an extraordinary sequence of events from 1992 onwards. A rising tide of legalism met and for a time engulfed the clientelistic practices of the Italian State. First, the national elections of April 1992 saw the ruling parties penalised heavily for their arrogance and corruption. The principal political beneficiary, at least in the north of the country, was the populist Northern League, headed by Umberto Bossi. His party, neolocalist and xenophobic, protested against the corruption of Rome in the name of a community of the North, hardworking and honest. The League wanted an autonomous northern Italy, and its taxes were to be fed back into services, not dissipated by the Roman bureaucracy. Sometimes 'autonomous' meant secessionist, at others federalist. In either case, the Risorgimento had been a bad mistake. Bossi's ideal community was a relatively closed one, deeply hostile to immigrants of any sort, whether extra-European or from the south of Italy. His message had a particularly powerful resonance in the economically dynamic world of small family businesses, which proliferated throughout the urbanised countryside of the North. In 1992 the League

1 For some indications, see Jeremy Tunstall and Michael Palmer, 'Media moguls in Europe', in Jeremy Tunstall (ed.), *Media Occupations and Professions*, Oxford 2001, pp. 67–8.

gained a startling 25.1 percent of the vote in Lombardy, 19.4 percent in Piedmont, 18.9 percent in the Veneto.

The mould of politics had been broken, to the benefit not just of new figures like Bossi, but also of reforming elements within the Italian State. Of these 'virtuous minorities', the one present in the judiciary was the most significant. For most of Italy's modern history, the judiciary had been firmly subservient to the executive, no more so than during the Fascist era. However, the postwar constitution of 1948 accorded the magistracy considerable autonomy, including the institution of a self-governing Higher Council. The Christian Democrats and their allies blocked the immediate realisation of the constitution's provisions, but by the 1960s the Higher Council was operating and a new generation of magistrates had taken up service. The judiciary was a corporation in its own right, jealous of its privileges, but the reforming elements within it, though never a majority, are a crucial element in the history of these years.

The campaign for legality in public life was directed and coordinated with great ability and tenacity by the chief prosecutor of Milan, Francesco Saverio Borrelli. A shy and reserved figure, but of steely determination, very much a Milanese bourgeois, enamoured of classical music and of horse riding, Borrelli was sixty-two years old in 1992, and had become chief prosecutor in Milan four years earlier. He came from a family of magistrates, and like Giovanni Falcone, the leading Sicilian magistrate who was to be assassinated by the Mafia in 1992, he had been deeply steeped in a culture of service to the State. Educated in Florence, he admired Milan for its 'European vocation, and its rather Protestant tendency to consider riches and success as a proof of divine grace.'[2]

---

2 See his long interview with the journalist M.A.Calabrò, *In prima linea*, Milan 1993, p. 6.

It might be supposed that such views would have led him to see eye-to-eye with Silvio Berlusconi, but the two men had very little in common, except perhaps their love of the city in which they both worked. Indeed, they represented two different parts of the Milanese bourgeoisie, and projected two diametrically opposite images of the city: the one, as we have seen, as the 'moral capital' of Italy, the other as the centre of a dynamic, modern but not necessarily very scrupulous capitalism. Borrelli's rigid and severe idea of a public sphere where there were clear and codified rules, no grey areas and no personal favours, was obviously an anathema to Berlusconi.

Borrelli's pool of magistrates in Milan, which included the famous ex-policeman, Antonio Di Pietro, moved with great speed and indeed ruthlessness in 1992–93. Their main target was corrupt politicians from the ruling parties, the Socialists and Christian Democrats in particular. Heads fell with great regularity. The most renowned of them was Bettino Craxi. In December 1992, he was placed under investigation for corruption, receiving and violation of the law on the public financing of political parties. As the charges against him grew more substantial, he fled the country in May 1994, seeking refuge in his villa at Hammamet in Tunisia, where he was to die in January 2000.

Corrupt politicians were the principal target, but businessmen's willing connivance with them was soon exposed. Senior management from FIAT, Carlo De Benedetti, the managing director of Olivetti, Raul Gardini of Ferruzzi, Gabriele Cagliari of the state-owned ENI, were all placed under investigation. Both Gardini and Cagliari committed suicide. Civil servants were also implicated. The San Vittore prison in Milan became the new, insalubrious *salotto* for those who had held power in the city in the 1980s. Milan itself had become '*Tangentopoli*', the city of bribes.

The example of the Milanese magistrates spread throughout Italy.

There was much to criticise in their actions from the point of view of the rights of defendants. The transcripts of their interrogations leaked out mysteriously, and were published by newspapers and journals. Public opinion was inflamed by the extent of the corruption that was being revealed, and it was sufficient for a person to be put under investigation for him or her to be considered guilty. In a country where concepts of honour and of cutting a good figure are very deeply rooted, the ignominy of public exposure was particularly hard to bear.

The prosecuting magistrates were intransigent and sometimes mistaken, but it would be wrong to conclude that they acted in bad faith. Nor is there any convincing evidence to suggest, as Silvio Berlusconi was to maintain relentlessly for more than a decade, that they were engaged in a left-wing conspiracy.[3] On the contrary; all the evidence points to the magistrates' political heterogeneity. Of the original pool of Milanese magistrates, Gerardo D'Ambrosio and Gherardo Colombo were on the Left, but Di Pietro and Piercamillo Davigo were both right-wingers, and Borrelli himself declared that his political inspiration derived from Benedetto Croce. What united them was their desire to attack widespread corruption and illegality. Overall, theirs was an impelling and indeed unique contribution to the relationship between Italian institutions, public ethics and society.

It was also one doomed to failure, reminiscent to the historian of the ill-fated Jacobin republics of 1796–99. The prosecuting magistrates were too isolated to succeed. After initial enthusiasm for their actions, public opinion became more tepid, alarmed that the enquiries would delve too deeply into all aspects of Italian life. 'Accommodations' and illegalities were too much a part of daily transactions for Italians to feel comfortable with an overzealous judiciary. Within the

3 This is the case made by Giancarlo Lehner, *Storia di un processo politico*, Milan 2003.

State, and amongst the politicians of the centre-left, the reforming magistrates found few real allies. The main opposition party, the Left Democrats, although only marginally touched by the enquiries, seemed to be too worried about possible skeletons in their own old Communist cupboard to give the magistrates the sort of political support they needed. Even amongst the judges themselves, as we shall see, there were elements deeply compromised by the system. The President of the Republic, Oscar Luigi Scalfaro, was on the reformers' side, but it was not easy to eradicate so consolidated a tradition of political and administrative corruption.[4]

2. La 'discesa in campo' ['Onto the pitch']

At the time, the Clean Hands campaign looked something like a political revolution, and indeed it was heralded as such by many commentators. Italy's ruling parties had effectively been swept away. A great void had been created in the centre of Italian politics, and it was into this space that Silvio Berlusconi stepped. By doing so, he attempted what no other media magnate had ever done before him: to unite very significant media ownership to national political power; furthermore in one of the largest and richest of modern democracies.

The reasons for Berlusconi's choice are complex. On one level,

4 The statistics of the 'Clean Hands' campaign tell a story of relative failure. According to the Procura of Milan, in ten years of activity, between February 1992 and March 2002, the courts had tried and passed definitive sentence in 1,121 relevant cases. Of these sentences, only 14.5 percent were of 'not guilty'. However, in another 46 percent of cases the courts had dismissed the defendants, mainly because the Italian judicial system had been too slow, and the time allotted for trying defendants had expired. Berlusconi himself was later to exploit to the full the snail pace of Italian justice; Gianni Barbacetto, Peter Gomez and Marco Travaglio, *Mani pulite*, Rome 2002, pp. 704–05.

the argument seemed a simple one. As he put it, employing inimitable footballing terminology: 'I heard that the game was getting dangerous, and that it was all being played in the two penalty areas, with the midfield being left desolately empty.'[5] With his friend and mentor, Bettino Craxi, disgraced, and with no other politician seemingly able to ride the storm – the popular Mario Segni, a reforming Christian Democrat, was clearly not up to the task – the only obvious solution was to step directly into the politicians' shoes.

On another level, there were impelling economic motives. From 1989 onwards, Berlusconi's Fininvest had moved dangerously and suddenly into debt. His was not the only media empire to find itself in trouble in these years. Rupert Murdoch, too, went through the stickiest patch of his long career in 1990–91, coming very close to succumbing to debt in December 1990.[6] In Berlusconi's case, excessive diversification was at the root of the trouble. In 1988 he had bought, at a considerable price, the Standa chain of supermarkets, one of the largest in Italy, hoping to become a major retailer of consumer goods as well as their principal publicist. A huge advertising campaign, based on 1,500 television slots, announced that Standa would forthwith become 'the home of the Italians.' It did not. The old-fashioned and unwieldy organisation, employing some 17,000 people, refused to be easily converted into the dynamic selling machine that its new owner desired.[7]

Fininvest had also diversified in other fields. In 1990, as we have seen, it had acquired the Mondadori publishing house. In the same year, Berlusconi bought the pay TV channel, Telepiù. However, by

---

5 E.Semino and M.Masci, 'Politics is football: metaphor in the discourse of Silvio Berlusconi', *Discourse and Society*, vol. 7 (1996), no. 2, p. 248. His other preferred metaphors were military and biblical.

6 Shawcross, *Murdoch*, pp. 349ff.

7 Madron, *Le geste del cavaliere*, pp. 182–4.

1994, it was reaching only 700,000 subscribers, far fewer than its French equivalent, Canal Plus, which boasted more than 3,500,000 subscribers at that time. Between 1987 and 1993 Berlusconi had increased his turnover fivefold, but his debts had grown twelvefold in the same period, and his profits diminished by more than twenty times.[8] He was in big trouble.

There was also the incumbent menace of a probable left-wing victory in the national elections of March 1994. At the local elections of the previous December, the centre-left had taken control of practically all Italy's major cities; even Naples and Palermo had fallen into their hands. The ex-Communists and their allies could with difficulty be considered a radical force for change, but the question of whether they would leave Berlusconi's commercial television empire untouched was certainly an open one.

Last but not least, it was not clear if and when the anticorruption magistrates would move against Fininvest. Many of Berlusconi's Milanese business associates had been brought into the investigative net during the previous two years. Borrelli recalled in 2002 that he had first met Berlusconi in the corridors of Milan's Palace of Justice on 17 March 1994, ten days before the national elections. Berlusconi had flashed his famous smile at the Chief Procurator. 'I am right in thinking there is no war between us?' Borrelli asked him. 'Absolutely right, for heaven's sake,' replied Berlusconi.[9] But both men must have known that it was only a question of time before their paths crossed again, and in different circumstances.

~

8 Giuseppe Turani, 'Non sono più d'oro le uova della Fininvest', *la Repubblica*, 12 February 1995.

9 'Memorie di un Procuratore', interview with Francesco Saverio Borrelli, in Baracetto, Gomez, Travaglio, *Mani pulite*, p. 689.

On 10 July 1993, a secret meeting took place at the villa of Arcore between Berlusconi and his closest advisors. Two of them, Fedele Confalonieri and Gianni Letta, a suave and moderate ex-journalist who was to try and mend many bridges in the coming years, were against any political initiatives. Marcello Dell'Utri, then at the head of Publitalia, was in favour. Berlusconi, with characteristic *élan*, chose to go ahead. In order to choose the name and the image of the new political party he employed all the considerable marketing, advertising and polling techniques of his organisation. Never in Italy had the creation of a political force been studied so minutely and scientifically, and never before had it assumed the form of a party so closely linked to a single business enterprise.[10] On 5 November the National Association of 'Forza Italia' came into being, and supporter clubs began to spring up throughout the country. However, it was only at the beginning of 1994, when the President of the Republic announced new national elections for the end of March, that Berlusconi took the final plunge. On 26 January, with a gesture of considerable symbolic importance, he sent a videocassette of nine minutes and twenty-four seconds, recorded at Arcore, to Reuters, the RAI and to his own television channels. In it he announced:

Italy is the country I love. Here I have my roots, my hopes, my horizons. Here I have learned, from my father and from life, how to be an entrepreneur. Here I have acquired my passion for liberty. . . . Never as in this moment does Italy . . . need people of a certain experience, with their heads on their shoulders, able to give the

10 Gianni Riotta, 'Il segreto della vittoria è "la strategia da judo"', *Corriere della Sera*, 30 March 1994; P. McCarthy, 'Forza Italia: the new politics and old values of a changing Italy', in Stephen Gundle and Simon Parker (eds), *The New Italian Republic*, London 1996, pp. 130–46; and the detailed reconstruction of Carmen Golia, *Dentro Forza Italia*, Venice 1997, pp. 27ff.

country a helping hand and to make the state function. . . . If the political system is to work, it is essential that there emerges a 'pole of Liberty' in opposition to the left-wing cartel, a pole which is capable of attracting to it the best of an Italy which is honest, reasonable, modern.[11]

In order to create this 'pole', Berlusconi allied himself with two very different forces of the Italian Right. One was the Northern League. The other was the Movimento Sociale Italiano (MSI), a party which sought its identity in the Fascist past and which was led by the young Roman politician Gianfranco Fini. He, too, after 1992 had seen a historic chance for the taking. His party, which had always been confined to the fringes of Italian politics, had a golden opportunity to move into the mainstream. When Fini ran for mayor of Rome in the autumn of 1993, Berlusconi endorsed his candidacy, and Fini polled 46.9 percent of the vote. In January 1994, he hastily set up an umbrella group with the name of Alleanza Nazionale (National Alliance), under whose auspices the MSI would fight the next elections. In time, National Alliance was to become a highly organised mass right-wing party in Italian politics.

The Northern League and the National Alliance were difficult bed fellows, and were to remain so right up to the present time. Fini and Bossi disliked each other, and their parties diverged radically. AN (Alleanza Nazionale) was strongly nationalist. Even if its evolution into a standard type of Italian political party developed

11 Silvio Berlusconi, 'Costruiamo un nuovo miracolo', *Il Giornale*, 27 January 1994. For a commentary on the speech and its staging, see M. Deni and F.Maresciani, 'Analisi del primo discorso di Berlusconi. Indagine semiotica sul funzionamento discorsivo', in M.Livolsi and U.Volli (eds), *La comunicazione politica tra prima e seconda Repubblica*, Milan 1995, pp. 227–41.

rapidly, its culture and party sections were infused with an overt nostalgia for a Fascist past.[12] Fini was to claim at this time that Mussolini had been 'the greatest statesman of the century'.[13] His was a party committed to the idea of a strongly centralised and interventionist state, with its support deriving mainly from Rome and the South. The League, on the other hand, was potentially separatist, racist but not Fascist, wedded to the free market but not to the national state. All three leaders – Bossi, Fini and Berlusconi – ruled supreme within their own parties. They were to fight democractic national elections, but there were few elements of democracy within their own organisations.

An alliance founded on such contradictory bases did not augur well for the future, but it served its temporary purpose magnificently. The election campaign that was fought between January and March 1994 was a rather one-sided affair because the media and other resources available to Berlusconi, when coupled with his whirlwind entry into politics, made for a very unequal competition. The progressive Alliance of the centre-left, led by Achille Occhetto, never really understood what had hit it. Berlusconi's campaign was quintessentially American, personalised and glamorous. The progressives pointed to his past career in the shadow of Craxi, and to his failure to separate business and political interests. Berlusconi replied by promising one million new jobs. He promised liberty from the state, from the Communists (real and imaginary), from excessive taxation.

The centre-right coalition achieved a remarkable victory in 1994. It obtained 42.9 percent of the vote in the Chamber of Deputies, which translated into 58.1 percent of the seats in the lower house. In

12 For the development of AN, see Marco Tarchi, 'The political culture of the Alleanza nazionale: an analysis of the party's programmatic documents (1995–2002), *Journal of Modern Italian Studies*, vol. 8 (2003), no. 2, pp. 135–81.

13 Alberto Statera, 'Il migliore resta Mussolini', *La Stampa*, 1 April 1994.

the Senate, its victory was less clear, and it fell just short of an overall majority, with 49.2 percent of the seats. But Berlusconi was confident that he could persuade a handful of senators to change sides, and that he had the numbers with which to govern.

His own party, Forza Italia, had gained 21 percent of the vote, much less than his pollsters had predicted, but enough for it to emerge as the largest political force in Italy's fragmented party system. Alleanza Nazionale had polled a very successful 13.5 percent, the Northern League 8.4 percent. At its beginnings, Forza Italia reflected faithfully the structure, values and personnel of Berlusconi's business empire. Some fifty members of the new parliament came directly from Publitalia. Here was the '*partito-azienda*' ('the party-as-firm'), an entirely new phenomenon on the western democratic political scene.

Michele Caccavalle, a bank manager from the Lazio region and neodeputy for Forza Italia, who was later to be disenamoured of the new party, has left us a valuable account of the party's inner workings at this time. He had been introduced to Forza Italia at Nettuno by the local manager of the Standa supermarket. Caccavalle was easily convinced that Italy needed a new centre-right party, 'a modernised Christian Democracy', capable of reforming a decrepit state, and of applying managerial pragmatism to Italy's economic problems. He found Berlusconi 'approachable – not an aristocrat like Agnelli, or a snobbish bourgeois like De Benedetti, but down-to-earth, affable, *simpatico*.' He went to Milan in February 1994 as one of the 276 candidates of Forza Italia. At the Teatro Manzoni (where Berlusconi had first met Veronica Lario) he received his '*kit del candidato*' (English terms have always been used with over-abundance in the Berlusconi camp). The kit cost each candidate one million lira (at that time about £600). It consisted of a luxurious bag 'full of surprises' – ties, adhesives, lapel badges, a videocassette with the party's programme, musical cassettes of Forza Italia's anthem to sing along to. Caccavalle found it 'all very kitsch and rather embarrassing', as well as expensive. Once in parliament, he was to discover 'that we Forza Italia deputies have not got a leader, but a boss.'[14]

3. Government and defeat, 1994–1996

Berlusconi's first government started well enough. At the June elections for the European parliament, Forza Italia increased its share of the vote to 30.6 percent. AC Milan won the European Cup.

Soon, however, the fragility of his coalition revealed itself. Far from running the State as a business, Berlusconi, hardly surprisingly, seemed out of his depth. In many key areas he tried to take decisive action, only to be forced to retreat. In an early initiative, he offered the post of Minister of the Interior to the very popular Milanese magistrate, Antonio Di Pietro. Berlusconi hoped in this way to circumscribe and limit the Clean Hands investigations. Di Pietro went to Rome, admitted to being seduced by Berlusconi's charm, but refused the post. On 13 July 1994 the new government passed a decree law, which basically intended to wind up the whole enquiry. However, the Milanese magistrates went on television to protest against this unwarranted interference, and even though it was the height of summer, the public outcry was immense. The Northern League's Minister of the Interior then backtracked and threatened resignation. On 19 July the government climbed down.

Other retreats followed. Pension reform was abandoned in the face of a huge trade union demonstration in November 1994. An

14 Michele Caccavalle, *Il grande inganno*, Milan 1997, pp. 10–11 and 42. See also Golia, *Dentro Forza Italia*, pp. 21–82.

initial attack upon the autonomy of the Bank of Italy, which had often served as an important check against arbitrary executive action, proved unsuccessful. The state bureaucracy had its own slow pace of march and self-protective agenda.

Worst of all, Berlusconi himself was drawn into the Clean Hands enquiries. On 22 November 1994, while he was presiding over a United Nations' international conference on criminality, he was handed a Notice of Guarantee, informing him that he was under investigation by Milanese magistrates concerning possible charges of corruption. The centre-right politicians and Berlusconi's televisions accused the magistrates of an 'institutional coup d'état'. According to them, there had been an outrageous attack upon the President of the Council of Ministers, at exactly the moment in which he was fulfilling one of the most important international commitments of his career. Certainly, the timing was not felicitous, as Borrelli himself admitted later. However, the charges were substantial ones, and formed part of a wider inquest into the alleged systematic bribing of the Finance Police in return for their turning a blind eye to false tax returns. I shall deal with these charges in detail below. In the following months, other grave accusations were levied against Berlusconi himself and members of his closest entourage, including Marcello Dell'Utri and Cesare Previti, Berlusconi's principal legal advisor and Minister of Defence.

By the beginning of December 1994 Umberto Bossi and the Northern League were no longer prepared to go on supporting Berlusconi. Many of the League's supporters still believed in the Clean Hands campaign, many more were on the side of the trade unions and against pension reform. Bossi felt he was being sucked into a highly uncertain parliamentary adventure which would deprive him of his mass support. He withdrew the League's ministers from the government, which duly fell on 22 December after barely six months in office. Berlusconi's first experience of high office had proved an ignominious affair.

~

For more than a year after his fall, Italian politics lived in a vacuum. The able and wily President of the Republic, Oscar Luigi Scalfaro, an old-time Christian Democrat but no friend of Berlusconi, refused to call fresh elections. Instead, he instituted an interim 'presidential government' under Berlusconi's former Treasury Minister, Lamberto Dini. Berlusconi himself complained bitterly: 'Democracy itself is at stake, that is if in the idea of democracy we include the right of the electors to express their opinions . . .'.[15] The polls were firmly on his side. However, Scalfaro was within his constitutional rights, and Berlusconi had little option but to sit and wait. On summer holiday in one of his luxurious villas in Bermuda, a youthful-looking Berlusconi, in white running outfit, was photographed leading out his obedient senior advisers, identically clad, uneasy and overweight, for their morning run. It was meant to be a very North American, presidential-style photograph, but there was something of the South American dictator to it as well.[16]

In this interim period, which was to last until the spring of 1996, Berlusconi's anger and sense of having been betrayed seem to have blinded him from seeing the contours of Italian politics. He failed to rebuild bridges with the League, or enlarge his coalition in any significant way. Antonio Di Pietro, afraid of being blackmailed and with an eye to politics, had resigned from the magistracy. He was, at the time, the most popular man in Italy, and definitely not of the Left. But Berlusconi was quite unable to entice him, or many other

15 Berlusconi, speech of 24 October 1995, in *Discorsi per la democrazia*, p. 126.
16 *Oggi*, vol. 51 (1995), no. 36, 6 September.

moderates for that matter, into his centre-right coalition. By contrast, the centre-left had reorganised in the Olive Tree coalition, and had found in Romano Prodi a very credible candidate for President of the Council of Ministers.

The April 1996 national elections were a very close-run thing. The Northern League chose to stand alone, equidistant from both of the major coalitions. It was rewarded with 10.1 percent of the vote, a notable performance which spelled disaster for Berlusconi in much of the North. Without the support of the League in Lombardy, Veneto and Piedmont, he could no longer aspire to that almost clean sweep of the uninominal seats that he had achieved in 1994. As a result, the Olive Tree coalition won a narrow victory. However, in the Chamber of Deputies it was dependent upon the unpredictable support of Rifondazione Comunista, the far-left party which had gained 8.6 percent of the votes in the lower chamber.

Berlusconi, who had waited with increasing impatience for these elections, thus saw power slip away from him. In spite of his continuing dominance of commercial television, he appeared to be 'yesterday's man', a meteoric figure but not one who had stood the test of time or fulfilled his own very considerable ambitions. The weight of judicial accusations continued to multiply. It seemed only a matter of time before Berlusconi exited from the scene, in one way or another.

4.   A family business.
Fininvest and the Financial Police

The trial of Silvio Berlusconi for alleged corruption of the Milanese Financial Police was just one of ten court cases which *The Economist* listed in April 2001 as decisive evidence of the fact that Berlusconi was 'unfit to govern Italy' for a second time. As he was eventually to be found not guilty and was to demand that the free press restore to him that 'honourability as a citizen and as a leader which has been trampled under foot',[17] it is worth following the terms and details of this trial as it unfolded, painstakingly slowly, at the various levels of Italian justice.

Everything began on 26 April 1994, when a young Vice-Brigadier of the Financial Police, Pietro Di Giovanni, went to see his superior officer, Colonel Guglielmo Miglioli, to tell him that another officer in the corps had offered him money which allegedly came from one of Berlusconi's companies. Miglioli told the young Vice-Brigadier to refer the matter immediately to the magistrates, which he did. Antonio Di Pietro took charge of the case, and over the next few months there emerged extensive evidence of the Financial Police taking bribes, in return for turning a blind eye to 'approximate' tax returns from a large number of Milanese companies. Fininvest was one of these. Three different occasions were identified in Fininvest's case, involving the sum of 330 million lira, or approximately £20,000.

Most of the firms involved sought to minimise the damage done to their image by adopting a policy of plea bargaining, admitting their guilt immediately and receiving reduced sentences in return. Fininvest resorted to a different strategy. While not denying that monies had been paid out, it claimed that the company had been a victim, not a perpetrator of the crimes in question. In other words, the Financial Police had subjected it to extortion threats. Furthermore, the com-

17 Berlusconi, 'Quell'attacco dei giudici che ha cambiato la storia', *Corriere della Sera*, 21 October 2001. He added that the Notice of Guarantee was 'the last of a series of public intimidations, completely alien to a State based on the rule of law'. His Minister of the Interior, Claudio Scajola, added, 'The winner is an Italy of progress, the loser he who wished to change the history of Italy against the wishes of the Italians'; D.Martirano, 'Berlusconi assolto, il Polo ora chiede le scuse,' ivi. See also Luca Fazzo, 'Berlusconi assolto va all'attacco. "Ora restituitemi l'onorabilità"', *la Repubblica*, 21 October 2001.

pany denied that its head, Silvio Berlusconi, knew anything about what was going on. Cesare Romiti, the Managing Director of FIAT, had adopted a similar attitude. 'How could I possibly know', asked Romiti, 'about everything that was happening in the company's eleven subholdings, which in turn control 1,033 companies?'[18] It was a line of defence that can be termed 'ignorance as a result of magnitude', and one often adopted by senior management in similar cases. The higher up the company, the less likelihood of knowing what was happening lower down. It was not a comforting line in terms of senior management efficiency or effective hierarchies of command and control, but it was a highly convenient one.

The defence strategy of FIAT and Fininvest differed in one key area. Whereas Romiti attributed total responsibility to the lower echelons of FIAT, with he and Giovanni Agnelli resting in blissful ignorance, Fininvest did not do the same. Salvatore Sciascia, the company's overall director for fiscal affairs, and a close collaborator of Silvio Berlusconi's – he and his family had often received gifts of money, watches and jewels from Berlusconi – admitted that he (Sciascia) knew what was going on, and that so too did Silvio's younger brother, Paolo Berlusconi. The admitted chain of knowledge thus ascended higher in Fininvest than in FIAT, reaching right up to the firm's family owners, but stopping just short of Silvio Berlusconi himself. This was just as well, because Berlusconi, as we have seen, was at this time President of the Council of Ministers.

Interrogated by the Milanese magistrates, Salvatore Sciascia confirmed the absolute dominance of the Berlusconi family in the company's structure: 'Fininvest is a holding which in substance is headed by the Berlusconi family. I mean by this Silvio Berlusconi, his

---

18 See Piercamillo Davigo's testimony to the authors of *Mani pulite*; Barbacetto, Gomez and Travaglio, *Mani pulite*, pp. 248–9.

wife, his parents, his sister, his brother Paolo Berlusconi and his five children.'[19] When it was his turn to be interrogated Paolo Berlusconi immediately admitted that he knew that monies were being paid, but that the Financial Police had threatened him with 'an unjustified expansion of their enquiries to include a meticulous control of formal irregularities.' He added that his brother had never been informed: 'The structure of the Fininvest group, leaving aside titular posts, has a precisely designated division of responsibilities: I personally manage all that concerns tactics and strategy, while Silvio Berlusconi has responsibility for the overall global strategy of the group.'[20]

Here the matter might have been forced to rest, at least as far as Silvio Berlusconi was concerned, had it not been for a peculiar incident that had taken place in June 1994, more than a month before Paolo Berlusconi had been interrogated. The Milanese magistrates discovered that Massimo Maria Berruti, a lawyer close to Berlusconi who had previously been employed by the Financial Police, but who was at the time an 'external consultant' for Fininvest, had left Milan for Rome on 8 June 1994. At 8:45 P.M. he had been admitted to Palazzo Chigi, the President of the Council of Ministers' official residence in the heart of Rome. A pass found amongst his papers demonstrated this fact. We do not know, obviously, the real content of the conversation between Berlusconi and Berruti, but little more than half an hour later, at 9:29 P.M., having just emerged from Palazzo Chigi, Berruti made a phone call to Marshall Alberto Corrado of the Financial Police. The following day, Corrado phoned another policeman, Colonel Angelo Tanca, with instructions to keep silent about one of the three episodes of alleged corruption that concerned

19 The Milanese magistrate's documentation of their case, including a number of interrogations, have been valuably reproduced in their entirety in Tribunale di Milano e Palermo, *Le mazzette della Fininvest*, Milan 1996. For Sciascia, see pp. 51–72.

20 Ibid., pp. 96 and 104.

the Mondadori publishing house. Both phone calls had been intercepted by the police.

This sequence of events, which came to light only in November of 1994, was sufficiently linear for the Milan pool of magistrates to begin investigations directly into Silvio Berlusconi. They duly sent him the famous Notice of Guarantee on 22 November 1994, as required by the Code of Penal Procedure of 1989, informing him of the fact that he was now formally under investigation. Besides Berruti's visit to Palazzo Chigi, there were many other elements which led the magistrates to doubt Silvio Berlusconi's defensive line of 'ignorance through magnitude'. From the confiscated official minutes of the meetings at Arcore of the 'Comitati Corporate,' which decided Fininvest's overall strategy, it became clear that Silvio Berlusconi, as so often happens with the heads of family firms, even very large ones, intervened obsessively on all sorts of minutiae: a salary increase for the manager, Urbano Cairo, the price of decoders for the pay TV channel Telepiù, the buying of a house for Antonio Craxi, brother of Bettino, a whole-page advertisement in *USA Today*, etc.[21] Was it really possible, the magistrates asked themselves, that he knew nothing of illegal payments, not of great economic size but morally very damaging for his company, and which were not a one-off phenomenon, but reiterated over time?

On 13 December 1994, Silvio Berlusconi, still Prime Minister, but only just, was interrogated by the Milanese magistrates. It was a dramatic confrontation.[22] Berlusconi began with a clarification:

In the document requesting my presence, I have read alongside my name the following phrase: 'the person who in fact at that time was in

---

21 Barbacetto, Gomez and Travaglio, *Mani pulite*, p. 281.
22 Tribunale di Milano e Palermo, *Le mazzette*, pp. 153–73.

control of the activities of the companies of the Fininvest Group.' I wish to state that this affirmation is absolutely unfounded. It is imposs-ible for any one person to have a real control [*controllo di fatto*] of the managerial and administrative activities of a group of these dimensions.

Francesco Saverio Borrelli insisted instead on the overall responsi-bilities of those at the top of Fininvest, and on the closeness of the links between Silvio and his brother:

Borrelli: 'Your brother has been defined as your *alter ego*.'

Berlusconi: 'No, my brother was not my *alter ego*. His role was as the person who was most easily accessible to everyone in the company, while I devoted myself to the other activities which I have described above. . . .'

Borrelli: 'From the episodes which are the object of the accusation and from other episodes, it is apparent that the Group had created hidden slush funds, to be used in certain circumstances. The 330 million lira formed part of these. Can you describe how these hidden funds were created, and with what modalities?'

Berlusconi: 'I prefer to call them "nonregistered funds", even if they were kept totally hidden from me. . . . I came to know about them only when these events came to light. I was very taken aback because, leaving aside my moral judgement on all this, which is absolutely negative, I consider such operations absolutely incon-venient for a group . . . which pays a billion lira a day in taxes. . . . You have to understand that 100 million lira represents one-thousandth of the daily operations of the Group, the sort of financial transaction which takes place in it every thirty seconds. . . .'

Towards the end of the interrogation, the magistrates concentrated instead on the role of the lawyer Massimo Maria Berruti:

Davigo [Piercamillo Davigo, another of the Milanese 'pool' of magistrates]: 'Did he [Berruti] explain to you that the reason for which he had been arrested was for having interfered with the course of justice by ensuring that the message [to stay silent] reached Colonel Tanca? This is especially important since our enquiries now show that this contact between Corrado and Tanca was triggered off after Berruti's conversation with you.'

Berlusconi: 'I deny absolutely that this contact can be derived causally, that is in a relationship of cause and effect, from my meeting with Berruti . . . I wish to add a final thing. It seems to me that nothing has emerged from this interrogation to demonstrate my direct responsibility in the three incidents that form the object of the enquiry. I hope you now are aware of the damage that this request for an interrogation has brought to me personally, to me as President of the Council of Ministers, and to our country, seeing that you sent me a Notice of Guarantee at the exact moment when I was presiding over the United Nations' conference on world crime.'

Davigo: 'Perhaps the terms of our last accusation are not clear to you. I beg your pardon and I will repeat them. The evidence shows that at 8:45 P.M. on 8 June 1994 the lawyer Berruti asked to have a meeting with you in Palazzo Chigi. A short time after, at 9.28 P.M., Berruti called a telephone operator and one minute later, at 9.29 P.M., he called the number of Marshal Corrado. The following day Marshal Corrado warned Colonel Tanca that he was about to be involved in the investigations and that he was to stay silent about the Mondadori episode. I hope that the temporal sequence of events and their weight as circumstantial evidence are now clear to you.'

In May 1995 the Milanese magistrates finished their enquiries and requested that the Berlusconi brothers, Sciascia and various members of the Financial Police be sent for trial. Berruti and Corrado were accused of aiding and abetting as well as of obstruction of justice. Three years later the judges in Milan gave their first ruling on the case. They found Silvio Berlusconi guilty and condemned him to two years and nine months imprisonment. But at the same time they found Paolo Berlusconi not guilty because he had taken all responsibility upon himself in order to protect his brother: 'It is not rare', wrote the judges, 'for the weaker suspect to take upon himself all responsibility, even at the cost of being condemned, knowing that in the event he can be sure of the gratitude of the stronger suspect.' The judges fully endorsed the prosecuting magistrates' thesis that Fininvest, not the Financial Police, had been the corrupting agent.

However, under the Italian judicial system, no sentence is enforced until the case has been heard at all levels of possible appeal. In the case of this trial, that meant both the Appeal Court and the Cassation Court, the highest level of Italian justice for nonconstitutional matters. In May 2000, the Appeal Court gave its verdict. It, too, condemned Silvio Berlusconi, but since the charges referred to incidents of nearly ten years previously, and since Berlusconi could benefit from a number of 'general extenuating circumstances', the statute of limitations came into play. The Appeal Court also expressed its doubts about Paolo Berlusconi's innocence, but since he had been acquitted at a lower level he could not now be retried unless there was fresh evidence against him.

Finally, the Corte di Cassazione gave its verdict on 19 October 2001, a few months after Berlusconi had again won the elections and returned to Palazzo Chigi. The highest court announced that the President of the Council of Ministers was not guilty. There was insufficient evidence to show that it was he who had been really responsible for what had happened. On the other hand, the court, though well known for the political conservatism of the majority of its judges, refused adamantly to accept the defence thesis that Fininvest had been subject to extortion threats. According to this definitive sentence, Salvatore Sciascia, Fininvest's Director of Fiscal Affairs, 'had certainly operated for the Group as a whole and not on the level of a purely personal initiative.' He had also discussed 'these matters on an equal basis with [the Financial Police], in order to obtain illegal advantages for the Group.' With the exception of Berlusconi himself, the Court reaffirmed the guilt of all the other accused, including the Financial Police and the lawyer Massimo Maria Berruti, who received an eight-month prison sentence.[23] Silvio Berlusconi was indeed found not guilty at the end of the day, but the circumstances revealed by the trial can hardly be said to have cast a favourable light upon the activities of his businesses.

23 http://www.osservatoriosullalegalità.org, Corte di Cassazione, sezione VI penale, sentenza 7 novembre 2001, n.39452.

4: RIGHT AND LEFT, 1996–2001

1. Retrenchment

F.Scott Fitzgerald wrote in his novel *The Last Tycoon* (1941), 'There are no second acts in American lives.' His axiomatic observation also held true in the torrid climate of Italian politics and business of the 1990s. After the seemingly interminable continuities of the Christian Democrat decades, when Aldo Moro could invent paradoxical geometric metaphors such as that of the 'parallel convergencies' to describe relations between Christian Democrats and Socialists, and when Giulio Andreotti could become President of the Council of Ministers no less than six times, the atmosphere of post-'Clean Hands' Italy was dramatically different. Elite instability, and even mortality, proved very high. Men came and went with alarming speed. By 1996, Bettino Craxi, Giulio Andreotti and Arnaldo Forlani, the three members of the seemingly impregnable 'CAF' of the late 1980s, all faced grave legal accusations. Craxi, as we have seen, had fled the country. But other politicians too, like the Christian Democrat reformer Mario Segni, hardly lasted a season. Even Achille Occhetto, who in 1989 had presided over the metamorphosis of the Italian Communist party into the Left Democrats, was unceremoniously sent on his way after losing the elections of 1994. As for the business world, as we have seen, in July 1993 both Gabriele Cagliari, the former president of ENI, the state-owned energy company, and Raul Gardini, Managing Director of Ferruzzi, committed suicide. Cesare Romiti, the very influential Managing Director of FIAT, was soon to be condemned for cooking the books of the great car production company. Only Giovanni Agnelli and Enrico Cuccia, head of Italy's most important investment bank, seemed to maintain a timeless quality about them.

Silvio Berlusconi did not appear at all immortal. In 1996 the belief was widespread that he too, having lost the elections, would shortly disappear from the political scene, and finish in the net of the Milanese magistrates. To add to his difficulties, he was diagnosed in May 1997 as suffering from prostate cancer, and was to undergo surgery for the condition. All seemed to conspire against his appearing for a 'second act'.

It is a measure of the man that he fought back with great determination and eventual success. Certainly, it would be true to say that he had no clear alternative. With the number of criminal charges against him and his associates increasing constantly, the chance of some sort of negotiated exit from Italian public life was very slim. He was going for broke, and knew it. Rupert Murdoch was interested in buying up his Mediaset television channels at this time. Berlusconi refused to negotiate, claiming later that his children had prevented him from selling up. This may have been true, but he knew full well that he needed both political and media power if he was going to survive.

Berlusconi thus had few options other than to stay in the front line. The way in which he did so, though, was little short of masterly. In a whole series of areas – legal, economic, party-political, European, coalitional – he retrenched with great skill.

The first battlefield was the judicial one, which from 1994 onwards was always to be his principal concern. In Italy, he was now being accused of illegally financing political parties, bribing the Financial Police, tax fraud, false accounting and the corruption of judges. In Spain, he was accused of tax fraud and the breach of antitrust laws.[1] One part of his defensive strategy appeared to be the postponement of judicial hearings for as long as possible, on the grounds that his political commitments did not allow him to be present. Delaying tactics of this sort, when combined with the very slow pace of the Italian judicial system, meant that there was a good chance of the trials being unfinished by the time the statute of limitations came into play. If this was Berlusconi's position, it was hardly an honourable way of clearing one's name, but there was every chance of it being an effective one.

At the same time, the 'organic intellectuals' of Berlusconi's television channels – those who had their own political programmes – began to launch a barrage of unceasing abuse against the prosecuting magistrates. This was a systematic media campaign, largely outside of the news programmes but inside the political sphere, which was to last almost ten years. It is difficult to estimate its full effects. The barrage was directed not just against the 'Communist judges' of Milan. As Marcello dell'Utri had been accused of links with the Mafia, and well-known politicians like Giulio Andreotti had been accused of colluding with it, the discrediting process was designed to encompass the anti-Mafia magistrates of Palermo as well. From the many examples possible, two will suffice to illustrate the history of this campaign. The flamboyant art historian and polemicist, Vittorio Sgarbi, who had become a Forza Italia deputy in 1994, had his own programme, *Sgarbi quotidiani*, on Canale 5 for a number of years. On 14 July 1994 he told his viewers: 'Di Pietro, Colombo, Davigo and the other magistrates are assassins who have killed people. They should be kicked out and no one would lament their going'. Two days later, he returned

1 'Silvio Berlusconi. An Italian Story', *The Economist*, 28 April 2001, p. 22.

to the attack: 'The judges of the Clean Hands campaign should be arrested, they are a criminal association with permission to kill, they aim to subvert the democratic order'.[2] Sgarbi's programme was usually broadcast more than once in the space of twenty-four hours. Paolo Liguori, in his programme *Studio aperto*, was also an implacable critic of the magistrates. Sgarbi, Liguori, Giuliano Ferrara, Emilio Fede, the anchorman of the Rete 4 news, preached the same unceasing message year in, year out: the magistrates were unreliable and vindictive, they were all left-wing, they had trumped up the charges for political reasons. A new 'video-truth' was thus created: Berlusconi was the innocent victim of a monstrous plot.

A second, crucial area of retrenchment concerned the economic bases of Berlusconi's empire. As we have seen, by 1994 Fininvest was in deep trouble. Excessive and precipitate diversification, as well as a reluctance to quote Mediaset on the stock market, and thus open the door to nonfamily capital, had pushed Fininvest dangerously into debt. The company's precarious financial state, as well as the need to preserve its near monopoly of commercial television, were amongst the strongest motives which had driven Berlusconi into politics. Yet while his political fortunes foundered in the fateful year of 1994, those of his company did not. Franco Tatò, a tough, independent-minded manager from Mondadori, nicknamed 'The Kaiser', was given overall control of the reorganisation of Fininvest. Although he antagonised a lot of traditional management, who recognised the authority only of Silvio Berlusconi, Tatò succeeded in carrying out fundamental reforms between 1993 and 1996. His insistence on the relative autonomy of the seven sectorial subholdings of Fininvest (Mediaset, Mondadori, Standa, Mediolanum, Medusa, Pagine Italia, Società Diversificate), meant, as Mario Molteni has written in his recent study of the the

2 Quoted in Barbacetto, Gomez and Travaglio, *Mani pulite*, p. 243.

Fininvest Group, that 'the sun had set on the typical organisation of a one-man company which had accompanied the development of the Group from its very beginning'.[3] In 1996 Mediaset was successfully quoted on the stock market.[4] The Standa supermarkets, which had been a heavy weight around the neck of Fininvest, were sold off, belying Berlusconi's boast that he never got rid of anything.

By 2001, the empire was back in good economic shape. It had not acquired a European dimension, and some of its owner's deepest ambitions, such as to control the cycle of the Italian consumption of commodities – from their advertising on television to their availability at mass retail outlets – had to be abandoned. In global economic terms, even in global media-enterprise terms, Fininvest was not much more than a bit player. Dreams of an international media empire had been abandoned, with only a 50 percent share of the Spanish Telecinco left outside of Italy. Nonetheless, Berlusconi was a very rich man indeed, one of the richest in Europe. His patrimony was estimated at this time at between 10 and 14 billion dollars.[5] This greatly increased wealth became the essential lubricant both of his own party and of the new political coalition which gathered under the name of the 'Casa delle Libertà', 'the House of Liberties'.

~

Other key developments in these years leant solidity to Berlusconi's political project. The growth and transformation of Forza Italia was one of these. The 'party-as-firm' was slowly transformed into a mass-membership organisation, the 'party of the people'. By its new statute

3 Molteni, *Il gruppo Fininvest*, p. 206.

4 For details of Mediaset, Berlusconi's media group, of which Fininvest holds 48.2 percent of the shares, see www. gruppomediaset.it.

5 www.forbes.com/finance/lists. *The Economist*, in its editorial, 'Fit to run Italy?', 28 April 2001, estimated Berlusconi's fortune to be as high as 'perhaps 14 billion dollars'.

of January 1997, Forza Italia was reorganised into an effective machine for mobilising electoral support, with a capillary presence covering the entire peninsula.[6] By the end of the year 2000 it had more than 300,000 members. The party had its strongholds in the three northern regions of Lombardy, Piedmont and the Veneto, which together accounted for more than 40 percent of its members. But it was strong too in Lazio, and in the southern regions of Puglia, Campania and Sicily. The statute of 1997 promised more power to the individual members of the party, in contrast to the top-down approach of its first three years of life. Yet there was little evidence by 2001 of democracy making much headway. The powerful 'regional coordinators' were still appointed by the President, and Forza Italia remained the personal fiefdom of Silvio Berlusconi, a 'personality party' in which idolatry of the leader was openly encouraged.

One of the greatest deficits with which Berlusconi had always to grapple was that of credibility on the European stage. He received bad European press in 1994, and worse was to come. However, between 1996 and 1999, he followed a patient strategy of presenting his party as the natural heir of the DC, with a view to gaining acceptance among the European Christian Democrats. His efforts were crowned with success in December 1999. Forza Italia was admitted to the EPP group in the European parliament. Romano Prodi, a Christian Democrat to his fingertips, was highly displeased, but Helmut Kohl and José María Aznar showed little hesitation in accepting the very useful 25 votes that Berlusconi had to offer.[7]

The last area of intervention, and the most crucial in electoral terms, was the re-establishment of the electoral pact with the

6 E.Poli, *Forza Italia. Strutture, leadership e radicamento territoriale*, Bologna 2001, table 8.3, p. 250. For the consolidation in 1997 and after, ibid., pp. 121ff.

7 Although not members of Forza Italia, Pierferdinando Casini and Raffaele Lombardo of the Catholic CCD are part of the Forza Italia group in the European parliament.

Northern League. Between 1994 and 1996, a truce between the warring parties of the centre-right had seemed absolutely impossibile; the odour of betrayal and the sound of Umberto Bossi's inimitable rhetoric were still too strong. Slowly Berlusconi realised that he could not do without the League. Giulio Tremonti, who was to become his Treasury Minister after 2001, a shrewd and very wealthy accountant from Sondrio, in the extreme north of Italy, patiently drew the Northern League back into the fold. Its support was on the wane, and Bossi realised that his best hope now lay in government and the patronage it offered. The North-South, centre-periphery split between the League and the National Alliance still remained, but Fini, not for the first or the last time, bowed to Berlusconi's wishes.

2. The centre-left

Between 1996 and 2001, Silvio Berlusconi came in from the cold, but he would never have been able to do so if the centre-left coalition which governed Italy in these years had not helped him along the way. If we return to the question of democratic antibodies mentioned in the Prologue of this book, to the degree of awareness and vigilance necessary in the changing conditions of modern democratic politics, we can see that the Italian centre-left suffered from major deficiencies. Its leaders had few of the qualities needed to confront so fast-moving, opulent and dangerous a player as Berlusconi. They offered no proper analysis of his rise to power. They were not clear, until it was too late, about the danger he represented. Though well-intentioned, they were overall less than resolute about the democratic ordering of the Italian state.[8]

8 'Democratic antibodies' are discussed by Paolo Sylos Labini, *Berlusconi e gli anticorpi*, Roma-Bari 2003.

Their record of government on the key issues here under consideration is a dismal one. No law on the conflict of interests was passed during the five years of centre-left power. No reform of the Italian media system was undertaken. No effective media authority was introduced to take the place of the toothless 'Guarantor for Telecommunications'. No strong line was taken on the incompatibility of Berlusconi's being simultaneously the leader of the opposition and under trial on a number of serious charges.[9]

Instead, Massimo D'Alema, the leader of the major left-wing party, the Left Democrats, tried to involve Berlusconi in a complicated process of constitutional reform. In January 1997, the bicameral commission for institutional reform came into being under D'Alema's presidency. This was the third such commission in less than twenty years, the previous two being those of 1983–85 and 1993. Both had proved resounding failures and there was nothing to indicate that the third would end differently. Berlusconi was primarily interested in his own fate. He was open to discussion on all manner of constitutional variations – semi-presidentialism, a German-style chancellorship, etc. – but the bottom line was very clear: there could be no deal without a castiron guarantee of his own legal future. When it was not forthcoming – the bicameral commission had no powers in this respect – he unceremoniously declared his opposition to the packet of reforms. After nearly eighteen months, D'Alema was left disconsolate and empty-handed.[10]

9 For D'Alema's defence on these and other issues, see his debate with the author of this book at Florence on 25 February 2002; 'D'Alema nella fossa dei professori', *L'Unità*, 27 February 2002; Concita De Gregorio, 'E il leader disse "Non c'è regime"', *la Repubblica*, 26 February 2002.

10 A first historical account of these events is to be found in Nicola Tranfaglia, *La transizione italiana*, Milan 2003, pp. 79–99. For D'Alema's viewpoint, see his *La grande occasione*, Milan 1997; and also Paul Betts and James Blitz, 'The FT interview. Massimo D'Alema', *Financial Times*, 22 December 1997.

Of equal gravity was the centre-left's attitude to the Clean Hands campaign. Although assuring formal support to the magistrates of Milan, and indeed to those of Palermo, the centre-left politicians were always reluctant to make the question of the respect of legality a central part of their political stance. They reacted on occasion and if pushed hard they would assure support, but they would never take initiatives. Of course, in the last analysis, the courts alone had the power to decide Berlusconi's fate. However, the government, as always in these cases, could help to create a climate of opinion: either to favour indulgence and procrastination, or else to encourage a situation where justice was being seen to be done. The Chief Procurator at Palermo, Giancarlo Caselli, at the end of his book written with his fellow-magistrate, Antonio Ingroia, about their experience in the Sicilian capital during the 1990s, posed a number of anguished questions about the centre-left's performance:

> Why was the possibility of increasing citizens' sensibilities towards the themes of legality, justice and the moral question put in doubt? Why was there no support for the concrete realisation of a new role for the justice system, truly based on equality before the law? Why was the new path which the magistrates wanted to follow . . . in the many inquests of the Clean Hands and anti-Mafia campaigns, interrupted and detoured?[11]

It was sad indeed that the Olive Tree coalition in Italy chose not to pursue these issues just at the moment when parallel scandals in Germany and France, involving Chirac when he was mayor of Paris and Helmut Kohl as Chancellor, revealed how much political corrup-

---

11 Giancarlo Caselli and Antonio Ingroia, *L'eredità scomoda*, Milan 2001, p. 175.

tion was a structural part of modern European democracy, and not one to be swept under the carpet.[12]

How is it possible to explain attitudes both so tepid and fateful? The answer is a complicated one. At the level of individual agency, Massimo D'Alema must bear considerable responsibility. A politician enamoured of *realpolitik*, very much in the mould of the postwar Communist leader, Palmiro Togliatti, he was convinced that he had Berlusconi where he wanted him. A weak and partially discredited leader of the opposition, with a very shaky legal record, was infinitely preferable to a new man with a clean bill, like the capable and popular Gianfranco Fini. Much better to leave him where he was than to call for his resignation. As Francesco Saverio Borrelli commented later, D'Alema was convinced that he had Berlusconi in his pocket.[13] He was wrong.

A deeply ingrained pessimism about Italian society also served to convince D'Alema that politics was a matter for elite compromise at Montecitorio, not mass campaigns or the mobilisation of civil society. In 1994, he had himself briefly been placed under investigation by Carlo Nordio, a magistrate from Venice. There was no question of personal corruption, but there was the question of his possible responsibilities in the illegal financing of his party by the cooperative movement. All charges were dropped, but the experience was traumatic and left its mark. D'Alema had no sympathy for 'overzealous' prosecuting magistrates.

He was not alone. The post-Communists in his party moved uncertainly on the terrain of the correct balance of powers within the State, and of that between the rights of defendants and the needs of justice. What was true of the Left Democrats was even truer of the

12 For the political corruption of these years, see D.Della Porta and Y.Mény (eds), *Corruzione e democrazia*, Naples 1995.

13 Interview with Borrelli, December 2001-April 2002, in Barbacetto, Gomez and Travaglio, *Mani pulite*, p. 699.

rest of the Olive Tree coalition. The political alliance which had defeated Berlusconi in 1996 was fractious and heterogeneous. Most of those who were in the centre of the centre-left came from a Christian Democrat past. They were opposed to taking any determined measures, either of a judicial nature, or regarding Berlusconi's predominant position in the media (the two issues had become almost inextricably intertwined by this time). For them, a policy of laissez-faire and letting bygones be bygones was the wisest one to adopt. Behind such attitudes lay a deep-rooted tendency in Italian political culture, clearly of Catholic origin, towards pardoning and forgetting.

The moderates of the Olive Tree coalition were scared, too, of losing precious electoral support. The resuts of a referendum of 1995, promoted initially by activists in civil society in order to limit Berlusconi's media power, seemed to confirm their worst fears. Italian voters had been called upon to decide whether the law should limit the number of television channels held by any one person. On Berlusconi's channels, the referendum was presented incessantly in the following terms: 'Do you want your free choice of evening viewing to be destroyed by the law?' The electorate had replied no, by 57 percent to 43, though whether it was responding to Mediaset's question or that on the ballot paper was no longer clear.

Throughout the Olive Tree coalition there reigned the fear of deepening that profound structural divide in Italian society which Berlusconi's rise to power had done so much to exacerbate. All those, and there were many, who believed primarily in freedom as freedom from interference, especially from State or judicial interference, lined up determinedly with Berlusconi. He delighted in using the term Communist in an all-embracing way, as signifying arbitrary state power, the deprivation of liberties, the suffocating of private initiative. These were evocative themes for a majority of Italians, and the centre-left was reluctant to leave too many such aces in Berlusconi's hand. It was better, so they argued, to lower the level of political tension, seek compromise, let things ride.

Last, but not least, they were comforted in such choices by the general political climate in Europe at the end of the century. The Italian centre-left had come to power in 1996, at a moment when the pendulum of politics in the major democracies of the western world had finally swung away from Republican and Conservative neoliberalism. The victories of Clinton in the United States, Blair in Britain, Jospin in France, and finally Schroeder in Germany, meant that the Olive Tree coalition had found a congenial and sympathetic international environment in which to work. However, the recipes for 'progressive' governments on an international level were heavily influenced by those of their predecessors. Reagan and Thatcher were long since gone, but the force of the neoliberal paradigm lived on in the minds and programmes of their opponents. The values of the market and of individualism continued to reign supreme: deregulation and privatisation, not only of industries and banks, but also of social services, went on apace, often well beyond the limits of previous conservative regimes. The public sphere became increasingly visual and increasingly passive, dominated by commercial television, to which public broadcasting was ever more subordinate. So great was the force of this model, and so widespread the fear of losing the middle ground of the electorate, that little progress was made in the elaboration of convincing alternatives.[14]

The Italian version of these general trends was a particularly hesitant one. The culture of the Olive Tree's reformism, with few exceptions, derived from that of the Bank of Italy — liberal, rational-

14 Perry Anderson, 'Renewals', *New Left Review* (New Series), no. 1 (2000), pp. 5–24; Colin Leys, 'Public sphere and media', *Socialist Register*, Rendlesham 1999, pp. 314–35. For a spirited rebuttal of accusations of insufficiency, Anthony Giddens, *The Third Way and its Critics*, Oxford 1999.

ising, watchful of the need to balance the books. These were important virtues in an Italian public sphere not noted for such qualities. But they were not enough. No corpus of left-wing thought emerged to complement and balance the intellectual weight of the liberal 'technicians' and intellectuals The centre-left governed from above, with reforms, norms and regulations being announced to an essentially passive citizenship. There was no attempt to build support and involvement from below, to create a climate of enthusiasm which could have sustained some of the government's worthier initiatives. In more than one sphere, as with educational reform and the teachers, exactly the opposite happened.

After Romano Prodi had led Italy into European monetary union on 1 January 1999, the centre-left lost its way. Giuliano Amato, who was to be the last of the three prime ministers of this period – Prodi had been the first and D'Alema the second – commented in March of 2001: 'If we've suffered from a defect in these years, it has been our inability to link satisfactorily the single chapters of our reform programme to a general design capable of involving the public, and of giving the perception of leading the country towards a better society of the future'.[15] The old Italian Communist and Socialist strategy of structural reform, the laying down of stepping stones to a Socialist society, had long since been abandoned, but nothing very distinctive had taken its place. By 2001 the centre-left said that it had governed well, and in some areas it had, but in the country there was scarse enthusiasm for, or even knowledge of, what it had done. The long-standing tradition which identified left-wing politics with the politics of participation and grass-roots democracy, of learning citizenship through practice, had been left woefully in abeyance.

15 Massimo Giannini, 'Le Cassandre sono servite' (interview with Giuliano Amato), la Repubblica, 2 March 2001.

3. The elections of 2001

By the time national elections were held in March 2001, Berlusconi was once again very much the front runner. His programme was a strong and simple one: decrease taxation, streamline the state administration, provide public works for the southern un- and under-employed; establish greater security in the cities, stamp out illegal immigration and its high co-relation with petty and not-so-petty crime; reform the judicial system and put an end to the prying and punitive actions of excessively independent magistrates.

His electoral campaign was fought with great opulence of means, which the lax Italian laws on electoral expenditure permit and even encourage. The lavishly illustrated booklet of 127 pages, entitled *Una storia italiana*, dedicated entirely to his entrepreneurial, sporting and political achievements, as well as to his idyllic relations with family and friends, was distributed to fifteen million Italian homes. It is a fascinating text. Written in what is a highly unusual style for Italian, with short sentences of ten to twelve words each, it makes exclusive use of those three to five thousand words which are the basic vocabulary of the language. Its structure is that of a series of fables. Each has a happy beginning, an immediate menace on the horizon, the collective struggle of a united group of friends ('Friendship, fidelity, loyalty, a taste for adventure, cheerfulness, intellectual curiosity: these are the characteristics of the "Berlusconi clan" '[16]), and an eventual triumph. The tone of the biography is that of inevitable, merited rise to power from humble origins. Difficult details are glossed over in a semifalse and sympathy-seeking fashion, as with the account of Berlusconi's separation from his first wife: 'The pro-

16 *Una storia italiana*, Milan 2001, p. 38.

fessional life of Berlusconi becomes ever fuller, with days and nights dedicated only to work. The family is serene, but something in the relationship with Carla changes at the beginning of the 1980s. Love is transformed into sincere friendship. Silvio and Carla, by mutual agreement, decide to continue their lives, with each one seeking their own fulfilment.'[17] The many fables of *Una storia italiana* are connected by the unifying theme of the fight of Good against Evil, of the 'Blues' of Forza Italia (blue is also the colour of the national football team) against the 'Reds' of the centre-left, of business Italy against the wicked magistrates: 'There was a terrible fear in the air, a grave preoccupation that the future of Italy would be an illiberal and suffocating one if the pre- and post-1989 Communists came to power. . . . The Procura of Milan had directed its cannons with great attention'.[18]

Television statistics reveal that Berlusconi had an overwhelming presence on his own channels, and a broad parity with the opposition on those of the RAI.[19] To personalise the campaign, Berlusconi insisted that his should be the only face on Forza Italia's hoardings. During the campaign it was thus possible to see this single, fixedly smiling face repeated thousands of times in the electoral bunting strung across the narrow streets of central Naples, or else the same face, enlarged beyond measure, staring solemnly downwards from the top of the pillars of a publicity temple erected in the atrium of Florence station. Such concentration of attention on a single figure was entirely new in the history of the Italian Republic.

17 Ibid., p. 11.

18 Ibid., pp. 70–1. For an interesting analysis of this text, Alessandro Amadori, *Mi consenta*, Milan 2002.

19 G.Legnante and G.Sani, 'La campagna più lunga', in R.D'Alimonte and S.Bartolini (eds), *Maggioritario finalmente? La transizione elettorale 1994–2001*, Bologna 2002, p. 59, figures 4 and 5.

Facing him was an uncertain, partially demoralised and profoundly disunited centre-left coalition. It was unable to regain the level of electoral unity that had brought it narrow victory five years earlier. Already in 1998 the fragile political truce had been sundered when Rifondazione Comunista brought down the popular government led by Romano Prodi. In 2001, the party of Antonio Di Pietro, the ex-magistrate 'hero of Tangentopoli', refused (or according to him 'was refused') an electoral accord. The 3.9 percent of votes that his party garnered were thus squandered and, as a result, many marginal seats were lost in the House of Deputies. Rifondazione Comunista, too, fought alone in the Senate elections, though not for the uninominal seats in the House of Deputies.

The centre-left thus joined the fray ill-humoured and program-matically ill-equipped. Even so, Berlusconi's victory was far from overwhelming. In the competition for the uninominal seats in the House of Deputies (75 percent of the total), Berlusconi's House of Liberties gained 45.4 percent of the votes against the 43.8 percent of the Olive Tree coalition. In the proportional competition (allotted the remaining 25 percent of the seats), the distance between the two groupings was much wider – 49.6 percent for the parties of the House of Liberties, 40.6 percent for the Olive Tree plus Rifonda-zione Comunista. Voters were clearly more willing to vote for a centre-left *coalition* than for its fractious component parts. In the Senate, the Olive Tree plus Rifondazione Comunista actually polled more votes than its opponents (44.2 percent against 42.9 percent). However, the absence of stand-down agreements cost them the chance of having broadly the same number of Senators as their opponents, a result which would have considerably limited Berlus-coni's room for manoeuvre. In the end, thanks to the workings of the new electoral law of 1993, the House of Liberties had a very comfortable majority in both houses: 368 seats against 261 in the

Lower House, and 176 against 134 in the Upper. The way was open for unfettered government.

~

It is perhaps worth making one or two observations about the connections between long-standing structural trends in Italian society and the pattern of voting in 2001. The unusually large and vital presence all over the peninsula of the self-employed, and more specifically of family firms and family shops, has never made the Left's task particularly easy, though there is no simple translation of the force of the self-employed into right-wing votes. As is well known, the central Italian regions have developed a dynamic tradition of small firms and industrial districts, without this jeopardising much of the left-wing electoral fidelity which has characterised them since the war.[20]

None the less, suspicion of a lackadaisical but occasionally punitive State, and the need to be free from its controls and above all its taxation, form part of the natural discourse of these sections of Italian society. The Christian Democrats understood this at a very early stage of the history of the Republic. The word *Libertas* stood at the centre of their political vocabulary and adorned the crusaders' shield which was the party's electoral symbol. Protection (pension schemes) and laissez-faire (a blind eye to tax evasion) were at the heart of their courting of the self-employed, both rural and urban. Berlusconi's 'House of Liberties' is the conscious heir of these traditions. In the elections for the House of Deputies of 2001, 63.4 percent of entrepreneurs and professionals voted for the 'House of Liberties',

20 Carlo Trigilia, *Grandi partiti e piccole imprese*, Bologna 1986; more recently Francesco Ramella, 'Still a "Red subculture?" Continuity and change in central Italy', *South European Society and Politics*, vol. 5 (2000), no. 1, pp. 1–24.

31.7 percent for the Olive Tree. The equivalent figures amongst shopkeepers, artisans and other self-employed workers were 54.2 percent and 34.7 percent.[21] That part of Italy which was instinctively entrepreneurial and individualistic, modern but vaguely Catholic, which had struggled in the course of half a century to found the material well-being of families upon hard work, self-sacrifice and a cock-a-snook attitude towards the state, recognised itself in the smiling face of the tireless little Milanese businessman.

Another strong connection between Christian Democracy and the House of Liberties, all to the detriment of the Left, lies in the long-term patterns of gender voting. After the war the culture of the Church and that of Italian women overlapped in a very strong way. It was with some trepidation that both the French and the Italian Left had agreed to universal suffrage in the period 1945–47. Nearly sixty years later, women over the age of fifty-five and those who are practising Catholics still show a very marked preference for the centre-right. However, the pattern of women's voting in the 2001 elections is not limited to this unsurprising fact. An extraordinary 44.8 percent of housewives – in themselves a significant social category, given the low percentages of female occupation in Italy – voted not just for the centre-right but specifically for Forza Italia. Furthermore, the more television women watched, the more they showed a propensity to vote for Silvio Berlusconi. 42.3 percent of those who watched more than three hours a day voted for Forza Italia, compared to 31.6 percent of those who watched only between one or two hours daily.[22] The connections between housework and the advertising of commodities, between the consumption of goods and the formation of subjectivities, between female viewing and the

21 ITANES, *Perché ha vinto il centro-destra*, Bologna 2002, p. 63, table 4.2.
22 Ibid., pp. 50–2.

packaged messages of the charismatic male political figure, are here to be found in striking form.

Against this, it is worth noting that women in work, those aged between forty-five and fifty-four (the 'cohort of '68'), and the youngest generation of women, eighteen to twenty-four years old, voted significantly in favour of the centre-left. However, it cannot be said that the Left has capitalised upon the favourable disposition of these sections of Italian society. In the context of the general misogyny of Italian public institutions, the Left in general has never waged a determined battle for equal opportunities, and the Left Democrats in particular are not seen as the party of female emancipation, however interpreted. The Ministry of Equal Opportunities remained woefully under-resourced and understaffed during the centre-left governments of the period 1996–2001.[23]

~

To these considerations of class and gender must be added those concerning regional tradition and development. A whole school of recent Italian historiography has taught us to beware of talking in terms of a single South, or for that matter of a single North.[24] None the less, the Left's historic weakness in much of southern Italian society has cost it dearly. For many decades, the experience of the Resistance in the centre-north from 1943 to 1945 was contrasted to the passive revolution of the Kingdom of the South in the same period. If the Republican cause prevailed narrowly over the monarchy

---

23 See the valuable testimony of the sociologist Laura Balbo, who was Minister for Equal Opportunities between 1998 and 2000: L.Balbo, *Riflessioni in-attuali di una ex ministro*, Soveria Mannelli 2002.

24 Above all the work of the academic journal, *Meridiana*; and Robert Lumley and Jonathan Morris (eds), *The New History of the Italian South: the Mezzogiorno Revisited*, Exeter 1997.

in the referendum of 1946, it was thanks above all to the voters of the centre-north, with some precious aid from the poor peasants of Basilicata and Calabria.

The rural and archaic nature of the South of 1946 has long since disappeared, but the structural weakness of the Left's vote has remained. Key southern regions, Puglia and Sicily in particular, were decisive for Berlusconi's victory in 2001. In a modernising process characterised by its pulverisation, by the distribution of cash benefits to individual families, high rates of youth unemployment, an uninterrupted culture of patron-client relations and covert political collusion with organised crime, the Left rarely found the themes or personalities around which a different version of modernity could coalesce. The recent and surprising exception of Antonio Bassolino, first the outstandingly popular mayor of Naples, and now the President of the densely inhabited region of Campania, suggests that this was not an altogether impossible task.

However, the Left's regional vulnerability is by no means confined to certain parts of the South. It now has a northern problem as well. Lombardy-Venetia, once the Italian pearl in the imperial crown of the Habsburgs, now the most economically dynamic and prosperous area of Italy, has rediscovered over the last twenty years a unity of economic purpose and of political persuasion that has effectively marginalised the Left. The Venetian provinces and many of the Lombard ones have expressed a dominant, though by no means single, culture of small family firms, conspicuous consumption and xenophobia. They have made an almost painless transition from being the fiefdoms of the Christian Democrats to the devoted followers of Umberto Bossi, and now from the Northern League to Forza Italia. The centre-left has been further emarginated. At the last election its parliamentary representation was reduced to the odd outpost at Trieste, the Venetian lagoon and the mountains of Trento and Belluno.

The crisis is not just a provincial one. Crucial to it has been the fate of Milan. Not that the commercial and banking capital of Italy had ever been the capital of the Left, but at the height of the Fordist period in Republican history (circa 1955–75) it boasted nearly 400,000 metalworkers in its immediate hinterland, concentrated in some of Italy's most renowned factories. In 1961 one in five of Italian metalworkers were employed in the province of Milan. Not by chance was the city twinned with Birmingham.[25] The rapid process of de-industrialisation after 1980, and the contemporaneous emergence of Milan as the headquarters of Italian high tech and of Berlusconi's television and publishing empire, radically changed the balance of forces in the city.[26] On the Left, the workerist ideology of old no longer had a substantive base in reality, and no fresh proposals emerged to replace it.

25 G.Petrillo, *La capitale del miracolo*, Milan 1992, p. 97. For a further breakdown of the statistics, S.Datola, G.Fajertag and F.Lissa, 'L'industria metalmeccanica mila-nese:1945–1975', in Istituto milanese per la storia della Resistenza e del movimento operaio, *Un minuto più del padrone*, Milan 1977, pp. 115–16.

26 Essential reading on these processes is Foot, *Milan since the Miracle*.

5: BERLUSCONI'S PROJECT

The temptation exists, and more than once in the twentieth century liberal and conservative European public opinion has succumbed to it, of not taking seriously personal projects for political dominion. Berlusconi himself, through his joke-telling and clowning at international meetings, his perpetual smile and expansive body language (right arm draped paternally around the shoulders of a colleague or friend), has tried to foster a particular image of himself outside of Italy, reassuring and dynamic at the same time. The endeavour has succeeded only in part, because for many participants in the European public sphere he remains the archetypical Italian – friendly and generous, lightweight and untrustworthy. Appearances, though, can be deceptive. His is a serious political project, drawing sustenance from some of the most profound changes in contemporary society as well as from the innovations of neoliberalism. He may well not succeed. The first half of his five-year term in office, as we shall see, has certainly not gone all his way. But the way in which he survived and then prospered between 1996 and 2001 should warn us against understimation or flippant dismissal. History, in any case, has taught us to be wary of little men with big appetites.

Berlusconi harbours ambitions for personal and charismatic control

of the modern democratic State. Such ambitions are not couched in
the language used in the frontal confrontations between dictatorship
and democracy in the first half of the twentieth century. Instead, from
both necessity and intent, he adopts the language of the American
empire, the universal values of liberty and democracy, justice and
prosperity, which lie at the heart of the United States' global project.[1]
This is the frame for Berlusconi's appetites, the confines of the
complicated passage of persuasion which he must work. In order to
do so, he has recourse to both the very new and the very old. He
brings to bear his profound experience of the modern techniques and
methods of mass communication, well aware of the degree to which
these are penetrative of the domestic sphere. At the same time much
of the content of his messages is far from new, but makes reference
to very long-standing cultural codes in Italian and Mediterranean
society.

1. Society, democracy and the media

The logic of democratic politics and the logic of television make
uneasy companions. Democratic politics depends upon lengthy and
complicated policy processes, upon the diffusion of power, upon
participation in decision-making. Its time spans are protracted and its
narratives often undramatic. It is sceptical of charismatic figures.
Television, on the other hand, at least as presently constituted, needs
personalities, 'current' affairs, conflicts, dramas and mini-dramas,
verbal duels. Its time spans are highly compressed and its narratives
archetypical. In the tension between the two, it is the logic of the
medium that has triumphed. Politicians of all beliefs adapt themselves

---

1 M.Hardt and A.Negri, *Empire*, Cambridge, Mass., 2000, pp. 17ff.

to its constraints, celebrate their television personae, practise their sound bites. The power wielded by leaders, carefully protected by their spin doctors and focus groups, has grown exponentially. At the same time, mass media markets have witnessed a dramatic process of concentration, both vertically and horizontally. Genre firms within each distinct medium have become ever larger; concurrently, there have been mergers between firms in different types of media, greatly facilitating 'cross promotion'. The contemporary media market is not made for minnows, and public broadcasting appears ever more a beleaguered outpost.[2]

The members of the global television oligarchy, of whom Silvio Berlusconi is a particularly fascinating example, are distinguished by a number of common traits: fierce attention to levels of audience share, upon which their life-blood, advertisements, depends; insatiable acquisitive tendencies; limited and conformist cultural frameworks. All this means that the medium is not safe in their hands. They may experiment occasionally and leave some editorial independence to their subordinates, but by and large they play safe, aim for high profits and produce television of a repetitive and unedifying quality, permeated by advertisements and selling techniques of every sort. The Italian case is not the worst. As one American reader wrote recently to the *Financial Times*: 'Unlike Italian television, we Americans can even choose among several 24/7 shopping channels, essentially 24/7 advertising, and many late-night infomercials and advertorials. . . . Despite the fifty or more channels available to the typical American cable TV viewer, the fare is mostly the same stultifying and mind-numbing drivel'.[3]

2 T.Meyer (with L.Hinchman), *Media Democracy*, Oxford 2002; G.Doyle, *Media Ownership*, London 2002.

3 B.Myers, 'Dissent that drowns in the din of TV drivel', *Financial Times*, Letters, 22 February 2003.

There is no iron law which dictates that all televsion, even all commercial television, need be like this. Potentially at least, the medium can have highly positive effects. In the 1960s in Italy, public television, in spite of its many failings, had performed a valuable educative role, informing parts of the population which otherwise had little or no contact with elements of a national or international culture. Joshua Meyrowitz, in a renowned study of the mid-1980s, argued that the levelling effects of the electronic media were also worthy of serious attention. They had led to a new 'situational geography' of social life, in which hierarchical senses of place and position had been broken down: 'through television rich and poor, young and old, scholars and illiterates . . . often share the same or very similar information at the same moment'.[4] The benign effects of television, however, depend heavily upon two crucial factors: who controls the medium and how culturally rich and varied is the society in which it operates. These two factors are closely interrelated, though the second is not entirely dependent upon the first. If control is too narrow and mass culture is lacking in autonomy and criticality, then the links between television and *civil* society will indeed be tenuous. This is exactly what is happening at the present time.

Private television is owned by the hyper-rich, by conglomerates and corporations.[5] It is run by corporate managers earning enormous salaries, but it is consumed by their social opposites. In the United States, Italy and elsewhere, families with the lowest level of education and of income are the most dependent on television. They most feel television as a 'physiological need', to use again Alberto Moravia's felicitous expression. They are also those least involved in civil society.

4 J.Meyrowitz, *No Sense of Place*, Oxford 1985, p. 90.
5 Informative of this world is Ronald V.Bettig and Jeanne Lyn Hall, *Big Media, Big Money. Cultural Texts and Political Economics*, Lanham 2003.

Passivity and privatism are not effective bulwarks against the dominant messages being projected at these families from television screens. Rather, they are those who are most likely to respond positively to the 'preferred reading' of the messages encoded in media texts.

~

It is within this context that we must examine the Italian case. By 2002 average daily viewing time per individual in Italy had reached three hours fifty minutes. In 1988 the equivalent figure had been nearly one hour less. Italians watched more television than any other nation in western Europe, though less than the United States. In 1996 Mike Bongiorno, Italy's veteran quiz show compère, commented on one of his programmes: 'The statistics tell us that Italian children of five to six years old watch television three or four hours a day and that old people watch even more. In Italy, we live for television, we take our arguments from it. Perhaps I'm exaggerating a bit, but it is like that. Anything we do, we do thinking about the television'.[6] He was indeed exaggerating, but he failed to mention one crucial fact. Ever since its inception, the great majority of commercial television had been run by his close friend and employer, Silvio Berlusconi. From 1983 onwards, all the major cultural choices and political attitudes of three national channels had been dictated by one man, who had also been President of the Council of Ministers in 1994, and who wanted to return to running the country as soon as possible. This was the Italian anomaly.

6 From Bongiorno's show *Telemania*, Rete 4, 11 December 1996, reported in Grasso, *Storia della televisione italiana*, p. 623. For comparative statistics, see www.mediametrie.fr. The US figure for 2002 is four hours nineteen minutes.

2. Family dreams

Central to the creation of a television culture of mass content is the question of consumerism, with its perpetual cycle of desire, acquisition, use, disillusion, rejection and then renewed desire. At the heart of modern consumerism, it can be argued, lies the enhancement of life through a greatly increased wealth of experience and personal choice, both in the realm of goods and of services. However, choice does not take place in a vacuum. The housewives who vote in such large numbers for Silvio Berlusconi, and who watch so much of his television, are bombarded with purchasing proposals at fifteen-minute intervals throughout the day.[7] Their children are subject to equally insistent advertising during their programmes, but with the volume automatically increased during the breaks for advertisements. Tilde Giani Gallino's work on Italian families at the beginning of the millennium reflects the results of such bombardment. In her study, children's drawings of themselves and their families make frequent and startling reference to their own shoes, usually sneakers, above all distinguished by the logo of Nike, Adidas or Reebok.[8] Supermarkets are often present in these drawings. In one such, the child has drawn her parents but not herself. In her place, standing between her parents, is the shopping trolley. Individual identity is thus formed and expressed, as never before, in the context of insistent advertising

7 In 1994, for instance there were 165,959 advertising spots on public television and 775,936 on commercial television.

8 T.Giani Gallino, *Famiglie 2000. Scene di gruppo con interni*, Turin 2000, esp. pp. 42–53. The study is particularly valuable as it charts transformations by means of comparison with a similar research published twenty years earlier; Id., *Il complesso di Laio*, Turin 1977.

messages, which are then translated and acquire material form in the world of shopping.[9]

With the advance of modern consumption, ever greater emphasis has come to be placed on what Colin Campbell has called 'modern autonomous imaginative hedonism'.[10] Central to this concept is the place of daydreaming and longing. The visible practice of consumption becomes just a small part of a complex model of individual hedonism, most of which takes place in the imagination of the consumer. Television channels and the Internet, videocassettes and video games, 'Walkmen' and CD players, to mention only the most obvious modern instruments, all play to this world of emotions and romance, of dreaming and imagination. Shifts in television advertising reflect the same trend. From a traditional insistence on the quality of the product and its beneficial effects on the consumer, advertising in Italy as elsewhere has come to concentrate ever more on the emotional and passionate element in communication. Advertisements have become as much about 'virtual' lifestyles as about real products. The individual is encouraged to cut loose. There arises the paradox of an invitation to absolute freedom and choice, extended by a television system of absolute conformity.

~

Consumerism, however, is only one pillar of this construction. A strongly normative aspect exists as well. This is no longer pushed down Italians' throats, as with Catholic propaganda in the early days of television; it has become subtle and cumulative. The advertisements, variety shows and soap operas of Italian television transmit a

9 For a complex and convincing treatment of these processes, D. Miller, *The Dialectics of Shopping*, Chicago 2001.

10 Colin Campbell, *The Romantic Ethic and the Spirit of Modern Consumerism*, Oxford 1987, p. 77.

powerful and continuous version of what Italian family values and life *should* be. The family is seen as a loving but also ambitious and even voracious entity, the site of enterprise and saving as well as of consumption. Ideally, it lives its daily life surrounded by a multiplicity of commodities: cars, cell phones, televisions, computers. Its values are tolerantly Catholic, vaguely inclined towards gender equality, but with mothers still playing a central role as providers of services: emotional, gastronomic, laundry and secretarial. It is further defined by reference to its shadow, as in 'reality' shows which concentrate on dysfunctional families or couples, much in need of the medium's magical reconciliatory powers.[11] The Italian television family is distinctly *familist* – in the sense of putting its own acquisitive instincts and interests first, and very rarely being portrayed as willing to sacrifice some part of these for the good of civil society, let alone the State. It is the incarnation of negative freedom.

In this sense, these imagined families belong to Berlusconi. They are neat, well turned-out, sporting, joking, computerised, pro-American, globe-trotting, business-oriented and privatised. They are, to use an Italian expression, profoundly *per bene*, in the sense of that term which signifies respectability, or at least the aspiration to be such. Of course, respectable and consumerist Italy existed long before Berlusconi did. But the crucial point is that he is its organic representative, the personification of the world of television advertising, of upwardly mobile dreaming become reality. Just before the elections of 2001, in the discotheques of Rimini and the Adriatic Riviera, young people told the journalist Paolo Rumiz that they would vote for Berlusconi because his television was full of young people, his party was a young one, he made them dream of success. Outside,

11 Some references are to be found in P.Abbiezzi, 'La famiglia "in" televisione', in M.Fanchi (ed.), *La famiglia in televisione. La famiglia con la televisione*, Rome 2002, pp. 35–51.

on the road between Rimini South and San Marino, Rumiz noted 40 hypermarkets in the space of ten kilometres, with cars queuing for up to 40 minutes to find a parking space.[12]

Berlusconi, then, is not just President of the Council of Ministers. Ensconsed in his magnificent eighteenth-century villa of Arcore, he also presides over the imagination of a consistent segment of the nation; not just those who already enjoy its considerable wealth, but also those who would like to, including large numbers of southern Italian families.

What is the nature of his charisma? It certainly does not lie within the canons of Max Weber's famous typology. If pure charisma for Weber was preeminently an extra-economic or anti-economic power, which at most 'can tolerate, with an attitude of emotional indifference, irregular, unsystematic acquisitive acts',[13] then Berlusconi can hardly be said to fit the bill. Nor would he fit that of Thomas Carlyle who, writing in 1841, was convinced that there were no modern heroes worthy of the name. Rather, wrote Carlyle, 'they are all as bank-notes, these social dignitaries, all representing gold; and several of them, alas, always are *forged* notes'.[14]

Berlusconi's money is real enough. Perhaps it is his charisma that is forged, in the sense of being constructed within the confines, practices and symbols of modern communication and consumption; carefully *manufactured*.[15] It is not that he is a particularly able orator,

12 Paolo Rumiz, 'Quelli del Grande Fratello "Con Silvio puoi sognare"', *la Repubblica*, 16 May 2001.

13 Max Weber, *On Charisma and Institution Building*, ed. S.N.Eisenstadt, Chicago 1968, p. 53.

14 Thomas Carlyle, *On Heroes, Hero-Worship, and the Heroic in History*, London 1901 [1841], p. 14. I am grateful to Stephen Gundle for drawing my attention to this quote.

15 Stephen Gundle, 'The death (and re-birth) of the hero: charisma and manufactured charisma in modern Italy', *Modern Italy*, vol. 3 (1998), no. 2, pp. 173–89.

nor physically particularly compelling, renowned for his heroism, or endowed with any other naturally charismatic qualities. For this reason he has long been underestimated. But he has worked with great care at creating and selling an image of himself. Pier Paolo Portinaro suggests three strands in this construction: that of the 'great communicator', careful to use simple language and attentive to all the details that make up a television frame; the 'master of evasion', not in the Houdini sense, but as the unrivalled salesman of escapist dreams; and the 'sporting fanatic', winner of trophies and munificent sponsor of a great football team.[16] These elements must, however, be preceded by another: that of the 'self-made tycoon'. It is his acquisition of riches, far greater than those of the late Giovanni Agnelli, long considered the richest man in Italy, that endows and enables the other aspects of his charisma. Berlusconi's opulent life-style, 'part-Dallas, part-Mediterranean chic',[17] may attract the scorn of some, but it is an essential element of his appeal. So too is that 'total love for himself' which Giorgio Bocca found 'at first disarming but then in the long run preoccupying'.[18] So great a concentration on one's own individuality corresponds well to the dominant ethos of modern Italy – best summed up by Berlusconi's own dictum of 1999: 'Individuals are their own best guides to what is good for them'.[19]

However, perhaps the essence of his charisma lies in its mirroring qualities. Many Italians look at themselves in the mirror – a national pastime – and imagine an opulent and powerful self reflected back to them. In the admiration for Berlusconi projection and self-recognition

16 Pierpaolo Portinaro, 'Sulla illegittimità del nuovo', *Teoria Politica*, vol. 11 (1995), no. 1, pp. 21–2.

17 Q.Peel and F.Kapner, 'Salesman on the spot', *Financial Times*, 23 March 2002.

18 Giorgio Bocca, *Piccolo Cesare*, Milan 2002, p. 11.

19 Silvio Berlusconi, 'Speech to the National Congress of the Forza Italia Youth Movement', Rome, 11 December 1999, *L'Italia che ho in mente*, p. 118.

are combined. This was clearly highlighted by Alessandro Meluzzi in the first number of Forza Italia's journal of ideas, *IdeAzione*. Berlusconi was one of those natural leaders who 'by their personal audacity or capacity end up becoming the symbol of the contemporary unstoppable mania for doing, moving, feeling alive. . . . A leader who will be chosen because everyone can recognise something of themselves in him, can identify themselves and that which they would want to be'.[20]

~

The production of consent via the media is a complicated process. It contains elements that are both of battering-ram insistence (the repetitiveness of the advertisements raining down upon us), and of considerable subtlety. The President of the Council of Ministers never misses an opportunity to observe that he is often criticised on his own television channels, and is even occasionally the object of satire, as on Italy's most popular regular programme, *Striscia la notizia* (Canale 5, 8:40 P.M.). How, in such circumstances, can we possibly be so foolish as to make a comparison with Mussolini?

At first sight this seems an impeccable position. Berlusconi has insisted on the pluralism of political voices on all news bulletins, another clear indication of his chosen adoption of the universalist language of liberalism. Recently his daughter Marisa, on becoming President of the Mondadori publishing house, the largest in Italy with 4,700 employees, and part of her father's empire, insisted that her guiding criteria would be 'profound respect for our readers and for the market, without any pretence to indoctrinate or orientate; the importance of a plurality of ideas and choices; an extreme attention to authors and to their possibility of expressing themselves

---

20 Alessandro Meluzzi, 'Sotto le ideologie niente, solo leader concreti e vincenti', *IdeAzione*, vol. 1 (1994), no. 1, p. 169.

freely'.[21] Beneath the pristine surface, however, things immediately become more complicated. Take the example of the eight o'clock news on RAI Uno, the flagship channel of Italian public television, where a formal pluralism prevails: every night there is a regular parade of politicians, among whom figure members of the opposition. They all say something briefly. After them, and sometimes before as well, Berlusconi or one of his ministers appears, to say something at greater length. There then follows the *cronaca*, mainly a series of depressing incidents and fatalities of varying nature. The Pope is given a ritual few minutes and it is time for sport. The general impression conveyed is of desperation at the state of the world, the vacuity of the politicians, the need for religion and the good sense of the Prime Minister and his government. Dissident voices from society are never heard. The multiple associations of Italian civil society simply do not exist, except when they become of such proportions that they cannot be ignored, as with the European Social Forum's peace march in Florence in November 2002.[22]

Berlusconi also makes reference, with some guile, to market shares for different audiences: left-wing voters must have some sympathetic television reserved for them, because this makes good commercial sense. His media regime is thus one based not on the silencing of all dissenting voices, as under Fascism, but on the rule enunciated with

21 R.Rho, 'Mondadori a Marina Berlusconi. Alla presidenza con orgoglio', *la Repubblica*, 19 February 2003.

22 These are subjective observations, based on faithful if long-suffering viewing of TG1 since Berlusconi's government took power in June 2001. They are supported by the statistics collected by the 'Osservatorio sull'informazione' of the Laboratorio per la democrazia di Firenze. Taking two days at random, 6 November 2002 and 11 February 2003, the time dedicated to the *cronaca* as described above was 45 percent in the first case, 42 percent in the second. Almost no time at all was dedicated to the associations of civil society or to dissident, non-party, voices. See also the alarming dossier on TG1 prepared by Usigrai, the journalists' union of the RAI; Jacaranda Falck and Stefano Livadiotti, 'Un TG davvero Cavaliere', *L'Espresso*, 22 May 2003, pp. 58–60.

acumen by the talk show compère, Maurizio Costanzo, in August 2001: 'Power does not belong to those who talk on television. It belongs to those who permit you to talk on television'.[23] When mass television audiences are at stake, Berlusconi's pluralism appears of uncertain quality. It was he who intervened directly in April 2002, from Bulgaria of all places, to announce that three major dissenting voices, Enzo Biagi, Michele Santoro and Daniele Luttazzi would be banned from the six television channels now under his (indirect) control.[24] When the trade unions called a general strike in October 2003 against the government's pension reform plans, they were denied adequate coverage of the strike on the RAI news bulletins. The President of the RAI, Lucia Annunziata, who had been appointed by the pro-Berlusconi Speakers of the two houses of parliament, denounced the government for 'using two weights and two measures' when broadcasting information.[25]

Italian television appears superficially as a reasonably plural, markedly repetitive and reassuring arena (variety shows and old films have always been very much in the fore). It has great appeal to an ageing population, but also to youth. In 1994, as part of a series of revealing school essays on new figures in Italian national politics, a Roman thirteen-year-old offered the following naïf and profound reflections on Berlusconi's media regime:

At school, almost all the teachers say that Berlusconi is a Fascist, that he'll sell the school to who has money to buy it. . . . But if Berlusconi

23 Maurizio Costanzo interviewed for Telegiornale, RAI 2, 28 August 2001, 8.50 P.M.

24 T.Fisk, 'Imagine if Blair tried to force Paxman off the air', *Independent*, 5 June 2002.

25 Natalia Lombardo, 'No ai sindacati su Raiuno, sì a Gasparri', *l'Unità*, 22 October 2003.

is a Fascist, why is he always laughing and happy? I learnt that the Fascists wore black shirts, were always in uniform, wanted the war and used their clubs on people. . . . And so they certainly had no reason to laugh, they were a gloomy lot. But if Berlusconi put on a uniform, started clubbing people and wanted to go to war, then his televisions wouldn't be watched by anybody'.[26]

~

The debate about the degree to which media control, especially television control, determines people's political allegiance and culture is a wide-ranging and complicated one. At an explicitly political level, scholars are deeply divided about the weight of votes brought to Berlusconi's cause by his media dominance. Such things are indeed difficult to quantify.[27] If we go beyond the political sphere to the deeper level of everyday life and of material culture, then the weighing process is even more complicated. As I mentioned in Chapter 2, it is essential to bear in mind the varying significance given to goods and services by consumers, and the complex way in which the powerful and repetitive suggestions of television are filtered by different families and individuals.[28] Even so, it is difficult to deny the

26 P.Nicotri, *Berluscon de' Berlusconi*, Venice 1994, p. 47. Nearly 1,000 essays were collected from eight different schools, from Luino in the extreme north to Palermo in Sicily.

27 In 1994 Luca Ricolfi, on the basis of an extensive investigation, argued that the influence of Berlusconi's televisions had been decisive in the national elections of that year; see L.Ricolfi, 'Elezioni e mass media. Quanti voti ha spostato la TV', *Il Mulino*, vol. 43 (1994), no. 6, pp. 1031–46. Other political scientists, such as Giacomo Sani, have been more sceptical. See his edited volume *Mass media ed elezioni*, Bologna 2001.

28 One in-depth British study concluded: 'There is no way of knowing whether someone who has his eyes glued to the screen is "viewing" any more intently than someone who is ostensibly conversing with his wife. Although the first person's eyes are on the screen, his thoughts may be far away, and while the second person's eyes are orientated to his wife, he may actually be listening to what is happening on the television'; P.Collett and R.Lamb, *Watching People Watching Television*, London 1986, p. 10.

over riding power of the connections that Berlusconi has established on his television channels and in his magazines over a period of twenty years: consumerism, advertising, family life, entrepreneurship, football, social mobility, charisma and political leadership have come together in spectacular fashion.[29]

4. Patrimony and the State

Buttressed by his control of the media, Berlusconi has turned his attention to the State. He intends, in the first place and as an absolute priority, to rein in the power of judicial review. He and his Minister of Justice, Roberto Castelli of the Northern League, insist that they are carrying through the operation in the name of greater judicial efficiency and the safeguarding of judicial autonomy. Such claims are rife in every area of the government's activity. In parliament the benches of Forza Italia are occupied in no small part by those who have worked in various parts of Berlusconi's business empire, and the lawyers who have taken his defence. The upper ranks of the state administration are, likewise, in the process of being renewed by a radical 'spoils system'. Fidelity to party and person, rather than precise criteria of professionalism and experience, is the guiding light of recent reform.[30] The CNR, Italy's funding institute for scientific

29 An interesting point of comparison, though less all-inclusive than the Italian case, is the reshaping of the Indian public under the influence of Hindu television soap operas and propaganda; Arvind Rajagopal, *Politics after Television*, Cambridge 2001. In this story, too, there is a significant consumption element, referred to as 'Retail Hindutva' ('Hinduness'), 'manifest not only in the range of consumer objects made available to new supporters of Hindu nationalism, but also in the variety of consumption styles and the range of modes of aesthetic appropriation possible' (ibid., p. 279).

30 For a convincing critique of the 'Frattini' law (no. 145 of 15 July 2002), see S.Ristuccia, 'L'Amministrazione perduta', *Queste Istituzioni*, vol. 29 (2002), nos. 125–6, pp. iii–x: 'We have melancholically returned to the the wars of investiture typical of the

research, has been placed under tight control by the Education
Minister, Letizia Moratti, who was briefly President and Managing
Director of Rupert Murdoch's News Corporation Europe before
accepting ministerial office. State schools and universities are being
starved of funds. The public health system, introduced in 1978 on
universalist lines, is being undermined by regionalisation and privatisation – reversing its trenchant defence by one of the centre-left's best
ministers, Rosy Bindi.[31]

If all goes well, Berlusconi himself is to move, at the end of five
years, from the post of President of the Council of Ministers to that
of President of the Republic. He aims to do so by direct popular
election, and in any case in the context of greatly added powers.
Once at the Quirinale, he will have reached the apotheosis of his
power; the sporting, joking, extraordinarily rich father of the Italian
nation. His role, as one of his sharpest advisors, Giuliano Ferrara, has
written, will come to resemble, of course with the appropriate self-
irony, that of Louis XIV, the Sun King.[32] Indeed in the early years of
Fininvest Berlusconi was frequently referred to as the Sun around
which the planets of his closest collaborators revolved.[33] Berlusconi's,
writes Ferrara, is 'a patrimonial conception of the State, in which

---

Middle Ages. . . . Each civil servant seeks the favour of princelings and princes, bishops
and kings' (p. viii). Ristuccia is careful to insist that the centre-left governments of
1996–2001 were far from immune to the idea of a spoils system, but that the provisions
of the 'Frattini' law constitute a further qualitative leap in the wrong direction.

31 The model here is that introduced by Roberto Formigoni, the President of the
Lombard region. It is based upon the state paying for services carried out mainly by
private (Catholic) hospitals, and upon the placing of privatised services in the hands of
cooperatives friendly with the regional government. Old-style clientelism and modern
privatisation are thus intimately linked. The centre-left regional governments of Tuscany
and Emilia-Romagna have remained closer to the original universalist model, and have
balanced their books more successfully than has Lombardy.

32 G.Ferrara, 'Prefazione', in P.Beaussant, *Anche il Re Sole sorge al mattino*, Roma
2002 (orig. ed., *Le Roi Soleil se lève aussi*, Paris 2002), pp. 12–13.

33 Molteni, *Il gruppo Fininvest*, p. 179.

public and private are indistinguishable'. The great man himself is an 'atypical figure symbolising a new power, despised, feared and adulated throughout Europe . . . Government is not to be separated from patrimony, nor the State from the person'.

How useful or accurate is it to talk of a modern patrimonial project at work in the heart of democratic Europe? In Weber's original formulation *patriarchalism*, in which authority within the *oikos* 'is exercised by a particular individual who is designated by a definite rule of inheritance',[34] gradually gave way in ancient societies to *patrimonialism*, in which personal, traditional authority became more extended spatially and dependent upon different forms of inter-personal relationships. Authority became 'decentralised'. The children and slaves of the household were settled upon the land, each with their own holdings, cattle and responsibilities, and the patrimonial leader gradually formed his own administration, 'a staff of slaves, *coloni*, or conscripted subjects', as well as 'mercenary bodyguards and armies'.[35] Naturally, decentralisation had its price. The followers and subjects of the patrimonial leader owed him absolute loyalty and military service, but he too owed something to them, 'not juridically but by custom, above all . . . protection in the face of external forces and help in times of necessity'.[36] A reciprocity of favours was thus established. In the economic field, patrimonialism leant itself to a wide variety of different possibilities, but 'the important openings for profit are in the hands of the chief and the members of his administrative staff. . . . There is a wide scope for actual arbitrariness and the expression of purely personal whims on [their] part'.[37]

34 Max Weber, *The Theory of Social and Economic Organisation*, ed. Talcott Parsons, New York 1947, p. 346. See also id., *Economia e società*, Turin 1999, vol. 4, pp. 106ff.
35 Id., *The Theory of Social and Economic Organisation*, p. 347.
36 Id., *Economia e società*, p. 107.
37 Id., *The Theory of Social and Economic Organisation*, p. 357.

Obviously, any transposition of such terminology into the modern world must be treated with the greatest of care.[38] We are not dealing in cattle or land, or with slaves, armed mercenaries and primitive chiefs. But the underlying mechanisms of power and personal relations delineated above have an extraordinary resonance in contemporary Italy. Personal authority and charisma (the latter no part of Weber's patrimonialism[39]), unlimited acquisitive ambitions and ownership, the arbitrary whim of the patron resting on a weakened rule of law, the reciprocity of favours, all these are cornerstones of Berlusconi's project. However, they are being pushed to the fore in a complex and democratic social and political system. It is one that has long since traversed, albeit more imperfectly than many western European societies, the stages of material and formal rationalisation. As a result resistances to such a project, as we shall see, are considerable, but so too is acquiescence.

~

It is worth noting, as many commentators have done, that there are also many populist elements in Berlusconi's self-presentation and political career. He is the person who, under the vigilant and doting eye of the long-serving political commentator, Bruno Vespa, went on television to sign a formal pact with the electors: if he did not realise his principal aims in the space of a five-year term of office, he would

38 The best discussion of such a transposition that I have found, albeit in pre-Berlusconi times, is that of Pierpaolo Portinaro, 'Personalismo senza carisma', which constitutes the preface to G.Roth, *Potere personale e clientelismo*, Turin 1990 (ed. orig. *Politische Herrschaft und persönliche Freiheit*, Frankfurt am Main 1987), pp. vii–xx.

39 As is well known, Weber's typology of power, of great articulation and historical sweep, is none the less composed structurally in an elementary fashion, combining and contrasting the criteria of personal and impersonal, ordinary and extraordinary, power. Patrimonial power, according to his scheme, is based upon personal and ordinary criteria, while charismatic power combines the personal with the extraordinary.

not stand again for re-election. He, too, when faced with the confirmation on 28 January 2003 that his own trial for alleged judicial corruption and that of his lawyer friend Cesare Previti were to be concluded at Milan, and not moved elsewhere, issued a videocassette from Arcore containing the following provocative statement: 'In a liberal democracy he who governs by sovereign will of the people can be judged, when he is in office and directs the affairs of State, only by his equals, by those who have been elected by the people. . . . Government is by the people and by who represents it, not by who has passed a public examination to become a judge'.[40] Mény and Surel's three basic elements of populist discourse – the celebration of the people's centrality and wisdom, their constant betrayal by the elites and the old political class, their necessary replacement by a new leader – are all present in Berlusconi's speeches.[41]

Yet it would be a mistake to confine his project within a populist framework, for that would be to miss much of its essence. The best biography of Berlusconi, though now a little dated, is that of Giuseppe Fiori, who chose as its title *Il venditore*, the Salesman. Berlusconi is certainly a consummate salesman, and a very well-prepared one.[42] But he is also, and probably above all, a *buyer* of commodities and services, of villas and footballers, of television channels and entertainers, of supermarkets and publishing houses, and much else besides. His is a patrimonial and acquisitive instinct, fired by the production and use of wealth, as well as the need for his name and face to be

40 P.Di Caro, '"Il governo è del popolo, non dei giudici"', *Corriere della Sera*, 30 January 2003.

41 Y.Mény and Y.Surel, 'The constitutive ambiguity of populism', in Id. (eds), *Democracies and the Populist Challenge*, London 2002, pp. 11–13. See also their *Pas le peuple, pour le peuple*, Paris 2000, and P.A.Taguieff, *L'Illusion populiste. De l'archaique au médiatique*, Paris 2002, pp. 117–21. Populism is also present as an analytical tool in Adrien Candiard's engaging *L'Anomalie Berlusconi*, Paris 2003, esp. pp. 223–4.

42 D'Anna and Moncalvo (eds), *Berlusconi in Concert*, p. 300.

omnipresent. In this respect, though not in others, he can be compared to a figure like Donald Trump, who liked to boast that he had the largest living room in New York and the city's most spectacular view. From the top of the Trump Tower, so his biographer recounted in 1993:

> [He] can see his name everywhere. In the air. On the water. And especially on the land. . . . Along the Hudson River between sixtieth and seventy-second streets lie the seventy-acre West Side yards, the largest underdeveloped real estate parcel in Manhattan, also known as the future site of 'Trump City' and/or 'TV City'. Across town on Third Avenue stand Trump Plaza, a thirty-nine story luxury apartment building, and Trump Palace, an even more luxurious fifty-five story apartment complex. . . . The Trump name is branded on a Monopoly-style board game called Trump, a TV game show called 'Trump card', a Brazilian horse race called the Trump Cup, a bicycle race called Tour de Trump, and a new custom-manufactured Cadillac limousine called the Trump Cadillac. It is in the title of his first book, *Trump: the Art of the Deal*, which remained atop the New York Times best-seller list for almost one full year. . . . 'I believe I've added show business to the real estate business', Donald told *Playboy*, 'and that's been a positive for my properties and in my life'.[43]

Here, at work in an ultra-modern setting, is an ancient appetite for unceasing personal accumulation and peacock display. In Berlusconi's case, more so than in Murdoch's or Trump's, there must be added the constant effort to create loyalty, and the need to be admired and loved. As Eugenio Scalfari once wrote: 'Silvio Berlusconi loves his clan and identifies himself with it. His greatest and most generous desire would be that his clan comes to comprise the whole of Italy.

43 Harry Hurt III, *Lost Tycoon*, London 1993, pp. 13–16.

Who enters therein can ask and obtain almost anything, who remains outside is an enemy or an infidel ripe for conversion. For him, television is an unrivalled business opportunity, but it is also the principal instrument for proselytism'.[44]

Such instincts and priorities, when combined with his plutocratic airs, do not make him a natural populist leader. At most we can say that populism enters strongly into his linguistic armoury, but that the material constitution of his project suggests the use of other terminology so as to define it better. Umberto Bossi, with his rough and direct language, regional base and grass roots social movement, fits the populist bill much better.

5. The legacy of the past

Apart from labelling, which is important but must not become obsessive, there is the question of origins. Much of Berlusconi's culture and activity are the expression of deep-rooted elements in Italian history. One of the most pervasive of these is patron-client relations. The survival and indeed predominance of vertical dyadic relations between patrons and clients in practically every sphere of Italian life, after more than fifty years of formal democracy, is as disconcerting as it is fascinating. In 1876 Leopoldo Franchetti, in his famous inquest on Sicily, described in memorable terms the qualities deriving from the *clientele* of that island:

> On the one hand, a fidelity, an energy in the friendship between equals and in the devotion of inferior to superior that knows no

---

44 Eugenio Scalfari, 'La breve avventura dell'arci italiano', *la Repubblica*, 15 January 1995.

limits, scruples or remorse. On the other . . . individuals who gradually group themselves around one or more potentate, whatever may be the foundation of his power: superior wealth and energy of character, or cunning, or other qualities'.[45]

In 1974 Pierre Boissevain published a book on Mediterranean anthropology entitled *Friends of Friends*, which explored the world of networks, manipulators and instrumental friendships.[46] In 1994 Berlusconi addressed his employees in the following terms: 'When I work with my collaborators I know that I will find myself amongst my best friends. . . . It is thus only just and indeed easy to create precisely at our place of work those moments of sentiment which are the most profound root of every feeling, the expression of friendship'.[47] Intimately linked with such attitudes is the practice of gift giving. Berlusconi is renowned for his largesse, which takes frequent and varied forms: a portrait of his family for the compère Mike Bongiorno; a free holiday for a wounded policeman after the G8 summit at Genova; wristwatches for the hostesses, firemen and *carabinieri* present at the NATO summit at Pratica di Mare in May, 2002. The virtues extolled in these practices are not those of citizenship but of devoted subservience, with little distinction made between the public and private sphere, between a prime minister and a patron, a civil servant and a friend or relative.

A second element is that of the *condottiere*. Berlusconi is a *cavaliere* of business, not of arms. Yet his is a martial approach to politics, based on high risk-taking and swift manoeuvre. It was these qualities which characterised his decision to enter politics in January 1994, and

45 Leopoldo Franchetti, *Condizioni politiche e amministrative della Sicilia*, Rome 1993 [1876], p. 40.

46 Pierre Boissevain, *Friends of Friends*, Oxford 1974.

47 D'Anna and Moncalvo (eds), *Berlusconi in Concert*, p. 302.

which gave him the impetus for an extraordinary victory just two months later. The image of the *cavaliere* is a potent one in Italian popular culture. Garibaldi and Victor Emmanuel II, often both on horseback, are ubiquitous in town squares. In 1994, as part of the same series of school essays quoted above, a thirteen-year-old from Bari wrote:

> It has been such a long time since they built monuments to famous personalities on horseback. Those that do exist are all monuments to famous people of the past. But now that there's Cavaliere Berlusconi, Head of the government and able winner of so many things, perhaps it's time for another equine statue. It could be of bronze or of marble, and he could be leading a courageous cavalry charge, crying 'Forza Italia!'[48]

These two elements, patronage and the *condottiere* tradition, if taken together provide the key to Berlusconi's masculinity. On the one hand he expresses a natural paternal authority, behaving as a truly Mediterranean patron, offering protection and rewards in return for loyalty and obedience. On the other, his is a constant assertion of a certain type of virility. Berlusconi presents himself as a ladies' man, not as a man's man, as Mussolini did, and his entourage plays willingly to this image. Marcello Dell'Utri told one journalist: 'Berlusconi has never been a libertine, but he is certainly a seducer, even if he has not had much time to dedicate to women. But when he puts his mind to it, he is uniquely charming. The seduction begins with his smile. He is a man who can make a conquest at first sight'.[49] And there is something of the feminine in Berlusconi's seductive charm, far

48 Nicotri, *Berluscon de' Berlusconi*, p. 22.
49 Ferrari, *Il padrone*, p. 27.

removed from habitual and brutal male conquest, which was very much the image that Mussolini projected of his masculinity.[50]

Virility, though, is not just a question of seduction. It is also a question of courage, of possessing '*le palle*', of having balls. To be a *cavaliere* of Berlusconi's stature, you have to have, metaphorically speaking, exceptional sexual equipment. He makes it clear that he is not one to wear the 'horns' of the cuckold. If anything, he will be the cuckolder, the giver of horns, not the cuckold, the receiver.[51]

These attitudes, adorned in modern vestige, come naturally to the fore in Berlusconi's dialogues. For example, at a meeting of Forza Italia at Udine in May 2003, he explained that the Cirami law, which had been introduced to allow defendants to protest against judges' biases, and to request the transfer of their trial (see below, pp. 144–45), was a sacrosanct piece of legislation. Why was this? The answer ran as follows: 'Who knows, perhaps one of us has stolen the fiancée of the presiding judge. Such things happen to us, because we're well known to be *tombeur des femmes*. . . . To steal the fiancée of a friend is not the sort of thing we do, but of a magistrate, well that's fine. [General laughter]'.[52]

Sometimes the talk gets dirtier, with undertones of sexual tourism and of the boys being in it together. One of his favourite stories appears to be of how early in his career he feigned knowledge of the extraordinary qualities of Circassian women's vaginas, in order to play along with a powerful client to whom he wished to sell the apartments of Edilnord. The scene is a train journey from Rome to Milan: 'I put

50 On Berlusconi's smile and the question of his femininity, see the perceptive article of Stephen Gundle, 'Il sorriso di Berlusconi', *Altrochemestre*, 1995, no. 3, pp. 14–17.

51 For a fine discussion of these themes in relation to masculine attitudes in a small Andalusian town in the 1950s, Julian Pitt-Rivers, 'Honour and social status', in J.G.Peristiany (ed.), *Honour and Shame. The Values of Mediterranean Society*, Chicago 1966, pp. 45–46.

52 Barbara Jerkov, 'Scippata la bandiera della pace', *la Repubblica*, 12 May 2003.

into action all my "charme" [sic], and when we got to Milan station, we were both still in the bar, half-drunk, with him telling me about the "nature" of Circassian girls. . . . We built up a friendship based on these common "cultural" bases, if you can call them that. He became my strongest supporter, my best friend'. Berlusconi adds that he had previously seduced his client's secretary so as to know what train he was taking and where he was going to sit.[53]

~

Of a different quality, but still very much part of a long-standing cultural tradition, is Berlusconi's constant and exaggeratedly stated respect for the Catholic church. All Italian politics, both of Left and Right, pass through the gateway of the Vatican City. For some, like Giulio Andreotti, the doors have always been wide open. For others, even devout Catholics like Alcide De Gasperi, the first leader of the Christian Democrats, they were partially closed. Togliatti tried to win the Church's acquiescence by forcing through, in the face of secular opposition, the continuation of the Lateran pacts in the new Italian Constitution of 1948. Berlusconi's version of these relations takes the form of state susbsidies for private Catholic schools, and support for as many of the doctrinal elements of the Church which do not contradict too glaringly his opinion polls and his own conduct. However, in the context of deep-rooted Italian culture, the most interesting aspect of the House of Liberties' Catholicism is its enthusiasm for one of the most archaic expressions of Italian Catholicism – the adulation of charismatic figures endowed with miraculous powers. Padre Pio, the Capuchin friar who is supposed to have

53 For two different versions of this story, both recounted by Berlusconi himself, see Ferrari, *Il padrone*, p. 25, and the much fuller version in D'Anna and Moncalvo (eds), *Berlusconi in Concert*, pp. 182–5.

received the stigmata, is the supreme example. In April 2000, Berlusconi's Canale 5 broadcast a two-part dramatisation of Padre Pio's life. Aldo Grasso, in his monumental history of Italian television, awarded it the accolade of programme of the year: 'The director Carlo Carlei has not spared us anything . . . where there was the possibility of exaggerating, he has exaggerated: rays of sun perforating the clouds, a photographic style taken directly from *ex voto* offerings, bleeding statues . . . burning bushes, furious battles with Evil which at times takes the form of a Molossian hound'.[54]

Lastly, it is worth noting that patrimonial attitudes to the Italian state are not entirely new. Leaving aside the Fascist experience, which was *sui generis*, one of the earliest Catholic critiques of the Christian Democratic regime, that of Ruggiero Orfei, was precisely that the party had 'occupied' the state.[55] The development of an independent administrative class, with its own codes of conduct and *esprit de corps*, was never the Italian State's strong point. The powers of discretionary conduct and service to the political class were always much greater. Even the judiciary enjoyed very little real autonomy before the 1960s. However, the Christian Democrat's occupation of the State was qualitatively different from that projected by Berlusconi. None of the DC leaders ever had the wealth or the media charisma that he has acquired. Most of them spoke to the people at great length in an incomprehensible *'politichese'*. Above all, none of them was ever allowed to become the acclaimed and undisputed leader of the party, and those who tried, as Amintore Fanfani and Ciriaco De Mita learned to their cost, came to a sorry end, victims of lethal interfactional plotting.

54 Grasso, *Storia della televisione italiana*, p. 694.
55 Ruggero Orfei, *L'occupazione del potere*, Milan 1976.

6. Berlusconi and Mussolini

How far are there echoes of a Fascist past in Berlusconi's personalist construction of power? Caution is obligatory in this field, for what strikes the historian immediately are the differences rather than the similarities between the two cases. What has been called the 'contrast of contexts' is here very strident, for the context of dictatorial rule in the 1920s and 1930s seems far removed from the mediatic and electoral democracy in which Berlusconi has asserted himself. Yet the two men do form 'a kind of commentary on one another's character'.[56]

It is very difficult to call Mussolini a patrimonial figure. His whole formation, as a militant Socialist and journalist, as well as his path to personal power, is strikingly different from that of Berlusconi. Denis Mack Smith, no friendly biographer of Il Duce, has written that 'it was perhaps strange that someone so adept at corrupting others with money had so little interest in wealth itself'.[57] Not that Mussolini was poor – his second autobiography, written in 1927–28, earned him over a million lira in its first two years, and another book he wrote in 1944 earned him a similar sum (this at a time when the President of the Council of Minister's annual salary was just 32,000 lire). But personal acquisition and ownership were not his driving spirits.

Patrimonialism, of course, is not limited to the question of the ownership of material goods. Patron-client relations were second

56 The methodological insight is Clifford Geertz's, working on a very different comparison; see his *Islam Observed: Religious Developments in Morocco and Indonesia*, Chicago 1971, p. 4. For the distinctions between comparative history as the parallel demonstration of theory, as the contrast of contexts, and as macrocausal analysis, see the excellent article of T.Skocpol and M. Somers, 'The uses of comparative history in macrosocial inquiry', *Comparative Studies in Society and History*, vol. 22 (1980), no. 2, pp. 174–97.

57 D.Mack Smith, *Mussolini*, London 1981, p. 108.

nature to both men, and the Fascist party, like Forza Italia, had such relations as their bedrock. Yet the reciprocity of favours was not a behavioural code that Mussolini espoused easily, for he considered himself above such things. Even more importantly, Berlusconi's refusal to distinguish between private and public interests, his concept of liberty as the individual's freedom from interference, his championing of private interests in areas previously the prerogative of the State, are all at the antipodes of the Fascist project. Berlusconi, as we have seen, wrote in 1999: 'Individuals are their own best guides to what is good for them'.[58] Giovanni Gentile and Mussolini had written in 1932, in their famous entry on 'Fascismo' in the new *Enciclopedia italiana*: 'Anti-individualistic, the Fascist conception of power is *for* the State; and it is *for* the individual only in so far as his interests coincide with those of the State'.[59] These are obviously two very different concepts of the bases of political power in the modern world.

The question of charisma also seems at first sight to mark a clear distinction between the two men. There can be little question that Mussolini made a very great impact upon those who met him, and not just on his sycophants. Winston Churchill not only thought him a good thing for Italy and Europe, but declared himself fascinated by 'his gentle and simple bearing and by his calm, detached poise', when he had his first meeting with him in January 1927. As late as December 1940, he continued to call Mussolini a 'great man'.[60] The

58 See above, p. 111, n. 19.

59 [G.Gentile] -B.Mussolini, 'Fascismo', *Enciclopedia italiana*, Florence, 1932, vol. 14, p. 847. For a sensitive comparison of the origins and context of the Fascist regime and of the Berlusconi government, Stuart Woolf, 'Crisi di un sistema e origini di una nuova destra. Senso e limiti di una comparazione', in Gianpasquale Santomassimo, ed., *La notte della democrazia italiana*, Milan 2003, pp. 50–68.

60 M. Gilbert, *Winston S. Churchill*, vol. 5, 1922–1939, London 1976, p. 226; W.S.Churchill, *The Second World War*, London 1949, vol. 2, p. 548.

English historian A.L. Rowse described going to hear him speak from the balcony of Palazzo Venezia in Rome in the spring of 1937:

> By and large he came out: a short stocky butcher, with a heavy ill-shaven jowl. He spoke with the hoarse voice of a Lansbury, the vocal chords worn out with much out-door speaking; but what struck me was the beauty of this ugly customer's ʃ   ʼres – there *was* something of the artist in him, of the artistry of his people.[61]

However generous one might wish to be towards Berlusconi, it is difficult to maintain that he has a charismatic effect upon those he encounters. Mussolini, in other words, fits more closely a Weberian idea of a genuinely charismatic figure, that is a personality 'set apart from ordinary men and treated as endowed with supernatural, superhuman, or at least specifically exceptional powers or qualities'.[62]

On the other hand, it must be remembered that Mussolini's charisma, like that of Berlusconi, was carefully constructed during the twenty years of his regime. Luisa Passerini has charted the successive layers of this creation of a myth, from its foundation in the period 1915–1926, to the 'exalting of his image' between 1927 and 1932, to the 'biographical explosion' between 1933 and 1939.[63] Berlusconi, so far, has had less than three years in power, though since the mid-1980s he and his consultants have worked assiduously on his self-presentation. We should try and imagine for a second, though it might cause pain to some readers, what 'exalting of his image' might occur in a hypothetical ten years from now, with Berlusconi having moved triumphantly from Palazzo Chigi to the Quirinale, and with

---

61 I. Kirkpatrick, *Mussolini: Study of a Demagogue*, London 1964, p. 155.
62 Weber, *On Charisma*, p. 48.
63 L.Passerini, *Mussolini immaginario*, Roma-Bari 1991.

the Constitution transformed so as to give him still greater powers as President of the Republic. In 2013 will the 'piccoli Forzisti' go to bed at night clutching in their small palms the medal of Silvio B., as the 'piccoli Balilla' did with that of Il Duce in 1935?[64]

64 See the illustration on p. 201 of Passerini's book, taken from M.Da Milano, *I ragazzi di Mussolini*, Milan 1935.

6. IN POWER

The translation of Berlusconi's project into political reality has so far been an uphill and accident-laden task. His government was sworn in on 11 June 2001. Of twenty-three ministers only two were women: Stefania Prestigiacomo at Equal Opportunities, and the redoubtable Letizia Moratti at Education. The Northern League was strongly over-represented in the new executive. Its electoral showing had been very poor (3.9 percent), but pre-electoral pacts were respected rigorously, for Berlusconi was haunted by the possibility of another rapid dissolution of his centre-right coalition, as had occurred in December 1994.

In the event, one initial motive for satisfaction was the solidity of the coalition. Many commentators were convinced that Fini and Bossi could not last long together around the same ministerial table. Too great were the distances between them in terms of culture, personality and electoral support: the one a cold and capable Roman politician, ex-Fascist, with his backing mainly from the South of the country; the other a loud-mouthed northern populist who sometimes preached the virtues of the Resistance. Instead they tried at first not to attack each other, both evidently enjoying power and fully aware that there was no alternative to their forced cohabitation. The new law on immigration (the Decree Law no.189 of 11 July 2002), a deeply iniquitous and racist piece of legislation, even bears their joint signature.[1]

However, relations deteriorated in the summer and autumn of 2003, with one part of Alleanza Nazionale deeply unhappy at what it regarded as Berlusconi's privileged treatment of the League. Bossi's plans for 'devolution', now at an advanced stage, may also lead to considerable tension. He wants all matters concerning health, schools and policing to be placed exclusively in the hands of the regional governments, and of their Governors in particular. Both Berlusconi and Fini are centralisers at heart, and must be reluctant to accord so much power to regional fiefdoms of this sort. In any case, Bossi's model conflicts with the strong Italian tradition of municipal government, and with the inevitable overlapping of responsibilities which characterise modern government in Europe. Increasingly, the League appears as archaic, racist and irrational – quite outside the usual political boundaries of the European Union.

1.   A spluttering economy

The centre-right coalition has just about held firm so far, but the economy has not. Berlusconi's project, inspired as it is by conspicuous consumption and the celebration of opulence, is especially dependent upon high levels of growth. Not only have these not materialised, but the Italian economy, in tandem with other European ones, has slumped badly in the past two years. Massive lay-offs at FIAT are only the most visible evidence of this extensive conjunctural crisis. Further-

1 For the law explained, A.Ballerini and A. Benna, *Il muro invisibile. Immigrazione e legge Bossi-Fini*, Genoa 2002.

more, the introduction of the euro has created serious problems of credibility, for prices have risen steeply in the wake of monetary conversion. Widespread scorn has greeted the insistence of ISTAT, the government's statistical office, that price hikes have remained under 3 percent per annum in the period 2001–2003. The net result of all this is that Italian consumption has dropped to one of its lowest points in the history of the Republic: an annual increase of only 0.4 percent in 2002, against a European average of 0.5 percent and an American figure of 3.1 percent.

Behind this very poor performance lies a graver structural problem. Many key indicators now point to the fact that the Italian economy is losing ground on a global scale. Its market share of world trade exports declined some 16 percent between 1994 and 2000. In the same period its gross domestic product (GDP) grew much more slowly than the European Union average. Research and Development spending is 1 percent of the GDP, about half the average of major industrial countries. Administrative burdens on start-ups are by far the most onerous of all the OECD countries.[2] Competitivity has slumped. Italy's largest companies, once rampant in the early 1980s, have performed dismally in the ensuing twenty years: Olivetti is now a mere holding company for Telecom Italia, FIAT, having once sold more cars than Volkswagen on the European market, is well on its way to becoming a regional unit of General Motors, and Parmalat has collapsed. There are exceptions, but they are not enough, nor big enough. As for Italy's myriad of small firms and industrial districts, more than once they have been given up for dead only to arise again miraculously. Their flexibility, design capacity and incremental inno-

---

2 For Italy's increasing structural weakness, see *OECD Economic Surveys, 2001–2002. Italy*, Paris 2002, pp. 30, 102–4, 106, fig. 26 and 27, pp. 123 and 127; L.Gallino, *La scomparsa dell'Italia industriale*, Turin 2003.

vations make one wary of predictions of imminent demise, but there is no doubt that the going has got tougher.[3]

In the face of these major problems, it is difficult to discern a coherent economic strategy emerging from the government, even within the narrow perspective of neoliberalism.[4] Confindustria, the Italian employers' association has grown increasingly impatient. In one or two cases, such as the raising of minimum pensions, electoral promises have been kept. But very many others have gone by the board: major infrastructural projects have hardly begun, and administrative procedures have not been simplified. At the same time falling tax revenue and low growth have been translated into major public spending cuts, which have rained down upon municipal government, social services, schools and universities.

A strong odour of crony capitalism pervades many of the government's economic initiatives. Within weeks in office, it had rendered innocuous the legal sanctions against accounting fraud, taking the opposite path to the United States in the wake of the Enron scandal. Fininvest itself had been investigated for cooking its books. Negative freedom has triumphed for the privileged classes in the form of tax amnesties – one such being that on undeclared capital illegally shipped abroad; another, more recent, aimed at reducing the heavy debts of

---

3 On the future of the Italian industrial districts, see S.Berger and R.M.Locke, 'Il *caso italiano* and globalisation', in *Daedalus*, vol. 130 (2001), no. 3, p. 93:

When one sees the fine garments being turned out in some of the Hong Kong owned plants in China by workers earning a small fraction of Italian wages, one wonders how long Carpi can hold out. Conversely, if it turns out that Italian small- and medium-scale district-based enterprises can prosper in global competition even in industries like garments and ceramics, then we need to revise expectations about the vulnerability of territorially embedded economic arrangements.

The authors' overall response on the Italian case is largely positive.

4 P.Onofri, 'Economia', in F.Tuccari (ed.), *Il governo Berlusconi. Le parole, i fatti, i rischi*, Bari-Rome 2002, pp. 153–68.

football clubs, amongst which is Berlusconi's own AC Milan. Inheritance tax has been abolished, a truly patrimonial action.[5]

Non-interference is also to be extended to the highly significant case of those who have constructed houses without building permits, a pervasive phenomenon in southern Italy, and one which has indelibly affected the southern landscape. Left-wing administrators of southern cities, such as Catania, had tried to combat the phenomenon by beginning demolition work. Berlusconi, on the other hand, intends to push through a 'more modern and positive norm', as he calls it, which would replace demolition with 'the obligation to realise a garden, contribute to a park or build a playground'.[6] Illegal constructions, which had reached a peak of 125,000 per year in 1984, had diminished to less than 30,000 by 2001. Their numbers have now begun to rise rapidly again, above all in Sicily.[7]

This high wave of dispensation, in the great Roman papal tradition, has done very little, as can be imagined, for fiscal compliance but much for a generalised sense of *laissez-faire* complicity with the government.

2. The police and the conflict of interests

Liberty, in the sense of the 'taking of liberties', was also to be found at work at Genoa in July 2001 during the G8 summit, in the now notorious actions of the Italian forces of order. As the magistrates' enquiry slowly unfolds, it becomes evident that the Italian police felt that they had a freedom to manoeuvre which they had not previously enjoyed. Whether this was a subjective reaction on their part, or the

5 The economist Marcello Messori counted at least fifteen types of tax amnesty in the 2003 Budget; 'Un programma per l'economia', *Micromega*, 2003, no. 1, p. 92.

6 G.L. Luzi, 'Abusi edilizi, stop alle ruspe', *la Repubblica*, 23 January 2003.

7 Ibid., interview with Ermete Realacci, President of Legambiente.

result of specific instructions, is not clear. In either case, what is clear is that sections of the police communicated to the demonstrators – whom they terrorised and even tortured in the Bolzaneto barracks, and whom they beat up in the Diaz school during their night raid of 21 and 22 July – that 'now our side is in command'. The principal evidence which the special forces used to justify this night raid – two Molotov cocktails – turned out to have been planted by the police themselves.

There is a very wide spectrum on which it is possible to measure national police forces, from the unarmed servants of the local community to the terror gangs of the South American dictatorships. In the Italian case many commentators, among whom must be numbered the author of this book, thought that the slow forward movement of Italian democracy had reached and deeply influenced even those areas of the Italian state historically most resistant to a democratic culture. From the basement of the Bolzaneto barracks came a strident negation of any such assumption. Here instead, alive and well, was a purely Fascist culture: Fascist in its slogans, in its brutality, in its wanton disregard for the most elementary rights of those taken into custody.[8]

In November 2002, in the run-up to the European Social Forum in Florence there were many fears of a repeat performance. A carefully orchestrated media campaign had declared the city 'too precious' to host such an event. The 'Black Bloc' was about to descend to destroy Michelangelo's David, Cellini's Perseus and much else besides. In the event a different model of policing prevailed: discreet, non-confrontational, cooperative. The replacement of the Minister of the Interior, Claudio Scajola, with a long-toothed Christian

8 The tales of horror which reached us did not just come from 'i ragazzi di Genova'. They also came from the reporters of conservative European newspapers like the *Sunday Times* and *El Mundo*.

Democrat, Beppe Pisanu, more used to the politics of collaboration, is one explanation for this shift. The good sense of the local prefect, Achille Serra, is another, while the collective pressure exercised by the Forum on potentially violent elements constitutes a third. However, there is no way of telling how long the 'Florence model' will hold. The structural problem of a police force which is to a disturbing extent deeply undemocratic remains unresolved. Nor is the government of the 'House of Liberties' likely to solve it, since unqualified support for the forces of law and order is much more its style.

~

Immigration, devolution, the economy, law and order – these are all standard priorities in contemporary European democracies. However, what is not is the personal patrimony and on-going trials of the incumbent Prime Minister. This great anomaly has occupied much of the Italian government's energy and that of public opinion.[9] It is a true indicator of Berlusconi's attitude to the relationship between private property and public responsibility that, more than two years after coming to power, no law on the conflict of interests (primarily his interests) has been passed by a parliament where he has large majorities in both houses. Back in June 2002, Pisanu promised the imminent realisation of the law, 'armed with a severe system of sanctions, as the opposition has requested'.[10] Little has been forthcoming. The government's draft law, left happily drifting in parliament, foresees the institution of a control authority with limited powers, whose head is appointed by the two Presidents of the chambers of

9 'It is as if this man has in some way to protect himself from the State at the very moment in which he has been called to its helm'; E.Mauro, 'Il conflitto di interessi che soffoca le istituzioni', la Repubblica, 27 February 2003.

10 R.Zuccolini, 'Dopo Natale il tagliando al governo', Corriere della Sera, 22 June 2002.

parliament, both of whom are at the present time members of the centre-right coalition. Article 2 of the law attempts a distinction between active control of an enterprise and the mere ownership of it, which is to be left in the hands of the proprietor. As the well-known liberal political scientist Giovanni Sartori has commented: 'The central question is that of power. In my personal library I have about a hundred books on the argument. Every single one of them explains that property constitutes power and bequeaths it'.[11]

A Roman lunch at the beginning of 2003 provides an instructive instance of the forms which Berlusconi's conflict of interests may take. On 12 February, Berlusconi, in his role of Prime Minister, entertained Rupert Murdoch at the Palazzo Grazioli in Rome. Present, too, was Fedele Confalonieri, Berlusconi's oldest friend and president of Mediaset. Murdoch's passion for pasta was satisfied with *fettuccine alla mediterranea* and *orecchiette alla cima di rapa*. The conversation over lunch, according to reports, concerned the future of Italy's television networks and, in particular, Murdoch's successful bid to create Sky Italia by taking control of the most important channels of Italian pay TV, Stream and Telepiù (2.3 million subscribers). Italian commercial television will now be dominated by a Berlusconi-Murdoch duopoly. In such a situation, so one would imagine, the role of an Italian Prime Minister is to identify what is likely to be in the best interests of the nation, and in particular of public television. But how can he, if he is simultaneously Prime Minister and proprietor of one of the two enterprises involved, and if his oldest friend is invited to lunch to represent the interests of that very enterprise? Afterwards Rupert Murdoch was escorted to the nearby Ministry of Communications. There the Minister, Maurizio Gasparri of the National Alliance, declared himself an enthusiastic supporter of the new project, which

11 G.Sartori, 'Quella vedetta è un po' miope', *Corriere della Sera*, 2 March 2002.

would 'take into account the tastes of the Italian public'. 'This will not be a colonialist television', the Minister reassured the journalists present. Murdoch's Roman tour finished with a brief visit to the office of the Guarantor for Telecommunications, an office hardly noted for the power or decisiveness of its interventions. By seven o'clock Murdoch was back in his private jet and on the way to London.[12]

Some months later he reassured the Italian public that the Italian system of information was a pluralist one. According to Murdoch,

> Mediaset broadcasts very little information in favour of Berlusconi, the RAI is securely anti-Berlusconi, and so is a significant part of the media. In America as well, press and television are against George W.Bush. But in any case, at the end of the day people make up their own minds.

This was a truly minimalist, though hardly unexpected, reading of how television influences people's minds and opinions. At the same time Murdoch promised to be a loyal competitor of Berlusconi's, and announced the constant expansion of his world empire: 'With American Direct TV, which also reaches South America, with Australia, Great Britain and Italy, we should have a base of some twenty-five million subscribers. And with India and China we hope to get to the figure of fifty million pretty fast'.[13]

~

If we leave Murdoch to return to lesser empires, the comparison with the United States makes for interesting reading. Michael Bloomberg,

---

12 See, principally, the detailed account by N.Lombardo, 'Rai, Baldassare non si fida più di Saccà', *l'Unità*, 13 February 2003.

13 Giovanni Pons, 'La ricetta italiana di Murdoch: farò concorrenza a Berlusconi', *la Repubblica*, 18 November 2003.

the present Mayor of New York, has a career pattern, personal wealth and electoral expenditure which bear a passing resemblance to those of Silvio Berlusconi. His business empire is valued at around 4 billion dollars, while that of Berlusconi was estimated at 10 to 14 billion dollars at the time of the 2001 election, and is now estimated by Forbes at $5.9 billion. Bloomberg has a large publishing business based in New York, with 8,000 employees, a radio station and a very influential cable television company, specialising in financial information for banks and stock market operators. He spent an estimated 60 million dollars on his election campaign, a sum which broke all previous records for New York elections. After he had won, *The New Yorker* commented: 'the contest proved that in politics, as in so many other realms of modern life, money trumps all'.[14] Like Berlusconi, Bloomberg presented himself as a man who would succeed as mayor because he had always succeeded in the past.

However, the Conflict of Interest Board subjected his private assets to the most severe scrutiny and made a number of pressing recommendations. For instance, all his shares that have anything to do with the affairs of New York City have had to be sold immediately. Nor are public attitudes to the culture of the taking and receiving of gifts the same as in Berlusconi's Italy. The Mayor wished to donate 'Bloomberg Terminals' to an under-equipped city administration. He was not allowed to do so. Such rigidity may appear excessive, but it depends on what store is set by public ethics, and how great the awareness is that even minor violations constitute the beginning of a very slippery slope.[15]

The US example is worth citing not because of any presumed

14 E.Kolbert, 'His Honor', *The New Yorker*, 19 November 2001.
15 F.Rampini, 'USA, conflitto di interessi. "Bloomberg venda tutto"', *la Repubblica*, 31 August 2002. In the New York case, the Conflict of Interest Board has only the power to make recommendations, but in reality Bloomberg has little option but to comply.

perfection in the regulation of its democracy. Its *laissez-faire* attitudes to electoral spending, for instance, have been disastrous. In 1976 the Constitutional Court ruled in the case of Buckley against Valeo that limits on electoral spending were a violation of individual candidate's freedom. Any such limits, according to the Court, represented 'substantial . . . restraints on the quantity and diversity of political speech [because] every means of communicating ideas in today's mass society requires the expenditure of money'.[16] No clearer constitutional invitation exists for economically dominant interests to buy up media space in order to determine the outcome of elections.

However, it is precisely the light and shade of the American system that serves as an interesting counterpoint to the Italian case. To what measure are different democracies equipped, as a result of their history, to limit and control modern patrimonial figures such as Bloomberg and Berlusconi? In what areas can the latters' great resources not be employed, which principles of public ethics are non negotiable, what barriers must not be crossed? These were questions posed by *The Economist* when it proclaimed, in a famous front cover and editorial of 28 April 2001, on the eve of the Italian elections, that Berlusconi was 'unfit' to govern Italy. Both his macroscopic conflict of interests and his highly controversial legal record, much of it still to be determined, ruled him out of play. *The Economist* was rewarded for its reconstruction of his business career with a pending libel suit for millions of dollars in the Italian courts. As one leading British columnist commented, this was a tactic which another media magnate, Robert Maxwell, had perfected in his time: 'Even if journalists believe a piece is impeccably sourced, lawyers warn about the enormous costs of an action . . . London wigs flutter

16 J.H.Birnbaum, *The Money Men: the Real Story of Political Power in America*, New York 1996, p. 34.

now when [Berlusconi's] name is mentioned'.[17] The risk of a libel case in a foreign jurisdiction, where the costs are all but unquantifiable, is far more frightening than one fought at home. And how free from the influence of the executive will the Italian judges be by the time the libel suit is heard? Such are the possible ways in which European public opinion can be curbed and restrained.

3.   Will justice be done?

In the nearly two years since *The Economist* published its inquest, the legal problems of Berlusconi and his clan have always received priority action in the centre-right coalition. Berlusconi himself, convinced that he is the victim of a judicial plot, has instructed his team of lawyers, who by January 2003 had cost him an estimated five hundred billion lire (his estimate),[18] to do everything in their power to safeguard his position in the key remaining trials. Most of his lawyers are members of parliament and even, as in the case of Gaetano Pecorella, the President of the Justice Commission of the Lower House. The greater the delay, the more chance for the statute of limitations (the expiry of the time allowed for the case to be heard at all three levels of Italian justice) to come into operation.

Various devices have been invented, some more successful than others. On 5 October 2001 the new law on international rogatories came into being. It renders more complicated the transmission and admission of legally relevant documentation from other countries – by demanding original copies of bank statements and trial transcripts,

17 N.Cohen, 'Britain isn't Italy . . . yet', *Observer*, 19 January 2003.
18 Reported in F.Verderami, 'Parte del Polo teme le barricate, ma il premier non esclude le urne', *Corriere della Sera*, 30 January 2003.

for example.[19] In December of the same year, Italy attempted to block the introduction of a European warrant for arrest for crimes such as corruption, fraud and the laundering of 'dirty' money. Berlusconi admitted candidly that he was disturbed by the prospect of such powers in the hands of a judge like the Spaniard Baltasar Garzón. The latter not only had requested the extradition of Pinochet from Chile, but had also brought charges against Berlusconi – for alleged tax fraud and the breach of antitrust laws regarding the activities in Spain of the television company Telecinco.[20]

On 31 December 2001, Roberto Castelli, the Justice Minister, attempted to transfer one of the Milanese judges sitting in the case concerning the sale of the publicly owned food company, SME. Both Berlusconi and Cesare Previti were accused in this case of having corrupted judges in 1986 in order to obtain a favourable sentence. Castelli's 'administrative' intervention was eventually blocked by the Court of Appeal. On 7 November 2002, in the face of widespread opposition, the Cirami law, named after its principal proponent, a Sicilian jurist, came into being. It reintroduced into Italian law the concept of 'legitimate suspicion': any citizen on trial can claim that there exists the legitimate suspicion of the court's non-neutrality, and ask that his or her trial be transferred elsewhere. It was on these bases that Berlusconi's lawyers requested that the key trials concerning their client and Cesare Previti be shifted from Milan to Brescia. The Milanese judges, according to them, were unlikely to give Berlusconi a fair trial since the prosecuting magistrates of the same city were so obviously biased against him; in Italy magistrates and judges form part of the same corporation, with overlapping career patterns.

Moving the trials to Brescia, with its concomitant delays, would

19 Article 18 of the law makes it operative for 'trials at present being held'.
20 Barbara Spinelli, 'Sotto sorveglianza', *La Stampa*, 9 December 2001.

almost certainly have led to the statute of limitations being enforced. However, in a dramatic sentence on 30 January 2003, the Cassation Court ruled that the trials of Berlusconi and Previti were to remain where they were.

Both the blocking of Castelli's attempt to transfer the judge in the SME case, and the ruling of the Corte di Cassazione on the question of 'legitimate suspicion', are indicators of distinct resistance, not just amongst prosecuting magistrates, but also at the highest level of the judiciary. I shall return in more detail to the question of such resistances, both institutional and other, in the last chapter of this book.

These resistances, though, are not consistent but fluctuating. Overall, it has to be said that if the outcome is uncertain, the pendulum in this terrible judicial marathon has swung in Berlusconi's favour. Soon after his election, the Cassation Court, in a crucial sentence, dismissed him from one of the trials in which evidence of alleged corruption appeared strongest, that concerning the Mondadori publishing house. For his part in this trial, and in the Imi-Sir case linked to it, Cesare Previti was condemned to eleven years imprisonment on 29 April 2003. As Previti was apparently acting on behalf of Berlusconi, questions would inevitably arise about the latter's alleged involvement. But this is a sentence only at the first level of Italian justice. Until such time as a definitive sentence is passed by the Corte di Cassazione, Previti goes free.

Above all, in June 2003 the government, having failed with all other expedients, hastily pushed a new law through parliament. It granted legal immunity for the duration of their tenure to the persons holding the five highest offices of the Italian state. In many other democracies, it is true, some legal protection of this sort is offered to the holders of high office, but the instrumental nature of the new Italian law was obvious to all. The SME case, in which Berlusconi was still one of the accused, had reached the summing up stage. The verdict was expected before the summer break. Instead, at the very last moment, the Prime Minister was granted immunity by his own government and parliamentary majority, and by the President of the Republic.[21]

Furthermore, once immune always immune. There is now little chance of his trial ever reaching a verdict, because one of the judges of the Milanese court, Guido Brambilla, is due to leave it in January 2004, without possibility of deferment, and under Italian law this means that the whole trial will have to begin again. In such circumstances, the application of the statute of limitations is likely. Berlusconi commented on 20 June 2003: 'My Calvary is over'.

At the time, more than 60 percent of the Italians were against any sort of immunity law, and even among centre-right voters only 25 percent were in favour of the law as it was passed. But it was also true that in the face of Berlusconi's unceasing propaganda war against the judiciary, public opinion took its distance from the magistrates; in the same poll, only a third of Italians still expressed faith in the judiciary.[22]

The immunity law was a decisive moment in Berlusconi's long legal struggle. The Constitutional Court has still to pronounce on the new law's constitutional legality, but even if it finds against it, it will probably be too late to conclude the one outstanding trial which the President of the Council of Ministers still faces; a classic case, if ever there was one, of shutting the stable door after the horse has bolted.

~

21 See Massimo Giannini, 'Ciampi salva il semestre europeo ma apre la corsa all'immunità', la Repubblica, 19 June 2003, and the splendid reconstruction of Ciampi's motives and political moves in the article by Giuseppe D'Avanzo, 'La miopia del calcolo', ivi, 20 June 2003. See also my comments below, pp. 165–67.

22 Renato Mannheimer, 'Toghe, crolla la fiducia. Ancora no all'immunità', Corriere della Sera, 19 May 2003.

The magistrates' lack of ductility has made the Berlusconi government ever more determined to carry through a radical reform of the judicial system. That it needs reforming is beyond doubt, for it is one of the slowest and least efficient in Europe. In addition, the prison system is bursting apart, with 50,000 inmates crammed into cells built for half that number. The judiciary itself, which was granted wide-ranging powers by the 1948 Constitution, must take its share of responsibility for the present state of affairs. However, what is at stake is not just a question of efficiency, or the mitigation of a brutal system, fundamental though both these are.[23] The Berlusconi government intends to bring the judges to heel, to destroy that autonomy which was the child of the 1948 Constitution, and which reached maturity from the late 1960s onwards. If successful, the government will undermine fatally the most independent judiciary in Europe.[24]

4. Europe and abroad

At the end of his first year in office, foreign policy was the field in which Berlusconi was judged most favourably by the electorate.[25] Initially, on the instigation of the President of the Republic, Berlusconi had appointed Renato Ruggiero, former head of the World Trade Organisation, to the post of Foreign Minister. After six months of bickering with his jealous, more politically oriented and euro-sceptical colleagues in the Italian Cabinet, Ruggiero quit on 6 January 2002.

23 For a severe indictment of the recent actions of the Italian judiciary, itself the product of 'a culture that discounted scruples', see Anderson, 'Land without prejudice'.

24 In November 2003, the magistrates held protest meetings throughout the country in order to explain to the general public the consequences of the new law.

25 Paolo Mieli, 'Governo Berlusconi: bilancio del primo anno', *Corriere della Sera*, 26 June 2002; Ilvo Diamanti, 'La Repubblica della sfiducia', *la Repubblica*, 4 May 2002; F.Borghignon, 'Berlusconi anno primo', ivi.

Berlusconi himself immediately took over the reins of the Foreign Office. For most of the rest of the year, until he ceded the post to Franco Frattini of Forza Italia, Berlusconi worked hard and with obvious pleasure at giving the Italians the impression that Italy under his leadership counted for more in Europe and the world. The synchrony of his views with those of the American President certainly helped him on his way. And the occasional gaffe, such as his famous remark about the superiority of western culture over that of Islam, appeared to do him no more than passing harm, at least amongst the majority of the Italian electorate.

Foreign affairs also allowed him to enter a new arena in which to project his not inconsiderable talent for image-making and fabulation. The NATO summit of 28 May 2002, at the military base of Pratica di Mare south of Rome, was an excellent case in point. Berlusconi went to extreme lengths to present the summit to the Italians as an exceptional historical event, marking the integration of ex-Communist Russia into the Alliance. At the same time he presented himself as having played a key role in mediating between the American and Russian leaders. Practically the entire Italian media, both video and newsprint, followed him in this representation of the event. The summit had been 'epoch-making', it had changed the 'course of the history of the world', Berlusconi had personally 'put an end to the Cold War', the meeting had crowned his 'titanic effort of mediation between the Great Powers'. All this had about it more than a little of the staged events of the 1930s.

It was only a shame, as the irreverent Italian journalist Curzio Maltese pointed out, that the rest of the world had not noticed the enormous significance of what had taken place. Of the twenty principal European and American newspapers, only one, the *Frankfurter Allgemeine* had judged Pratica di Mare worthy of the front page. In none of them was there any reference to the fundamental role of

Silvio Berlusconi. Of greater interest for nearly all of them, as far as Italy was concerned, was the crisis at FIAT. For the Americans what mattered was the meeting of George W. Bush with the Pope and the scandal of paedophiliac Catholic priests.[26]

In foreign affairs, an area where verification is hard to come by, the ability to fabulate to a mainly captive audience has sustained Berlusconi's government well. But with the approach of war, not even his formidable domestic propaganda machine could mask the contradictions of his policy. His subservient relationship with Bush, and Italy's long-standing Atlanticist policies, made the country an early member of the 'Coalition of the Willing' in the assault on Iraq, and Berlusconi a signatory of the pro-war 'United We Stand' letter to the *Wall Street Journal* of 30 January 2003.[27] However, such a stance flew in the face of very strong Catholic feeling and, sin of all sins, the opinion polls – which, in February 2002, registered a nearly 90 percent opposition to war. Berlusconi's support became distinctly more *sotto voce*. In the end he declared Italy to be non-belligerent – Article 11 of the Italian Constitution explicity repudiates war as a means of resolving international controversies – while at the same time 'supportive' of the Anglo-American war effort; a contorted position, to say the least. As in Germany's case, all facilities remained at the Americans' disposal, and the Vicenza base in north-east Italy provided the jump-off point for the US paratroopers who landed in northern Iraq in the last week of March 2003. Later, Italian troops

26 Curzio Maltese, 'La NATO e Berlusconi, una fiaba italiana', *la Repubblica*, 30 May 2002; P. Di Caro, 'La gioia di Berlusconi: "Tutto merito nostro"', *Corriere della Sera*, 29 May 2002.

27 On visiting the United States in July 2003, Berlusconi took part in Bush's daily intelligence briefing. He told reporters: 'I thought how important it was for citizens in the West to know with what attention, spirit of sacrifice and generosity the President takes into account all those developments in the world which could lead to a threat to peace and stability'; www.forza-italia.it, 21 July 2003.

were to be sent to Iraq as part of the American-organised 'peace-keeping' mission, and in November the *carabinieri*'s headquarters in Nassiyria was blown up, with great loss of life. United national mourning could not mask the contradictions of the country's foreign policy. No Blair or even Aznar, Berlusconi's domestic ability for swift manoeuvre and high risk-taking have not transferred themselves easily to the international stage.

~

With regard to Europe, the discourse is rather different. Berlusconi would like to change his country's traditional European policy. For many years Italy has been content to be in the shadow of France and Germany, sometimes performing a valuable role of mediation, but little else. Often she has been simply absent, her politicians much more concerned with Roman politics than those of Brussels. Even when present, Italy has generally reacted to Franco-German initiatives, rather than making proposals in her own right.[28]

There are distinct signs that this is no longer the case. Berlusconi intends to fight Italy's corner harder, on issues such as milk quotas and the siting of a European food agency. He is well aware of the opinions of euro-sceptics in his Cabinet like Giulio Tremonti, Treasury Minister, and Antonio Martino, Defence Minister, both admirers of Lady Thatcher — as indeed is Berlusconi himself. He is in favour of radical enlargement of the Union, even to include Russia and Israel. Vladimir Putin has become a close friend, and holidayed with Berlusconi in one of his Sardinian villas in the summer of 2003. The really important alliances, though, are with George W. Bush and Tony Blair. Not only does Berlusconi express a natural sympathy for

---

28 For a brief history of Italy's rather chequered contribution to the European Union, see Ginsborg, *Italy and its Discontents*, pp. 239–48.

the Bush-Blair axis and Anglo-American global perspectives. He is also keen on following Blair in importing these views into the heart of Europe. On issues like flexible labour markets and the privatisation of social services, Blair and Berlusconi are in close agreement. So, too, are the Spanish Christian Democrats, ably represented over the past years by José María Aznar. Berlusconi would like to forge a new axis, British and Mediterranean, to counter the historic Franco-German one, currently represented by Jacques Chirac and Gerhard Schroeder. Neither Chirac nor Schroeder seem able to hide their dislike of Berlusconi and distaste for what he represents. Blair and most of British New Labour, on the other hand, seem to have no such problems. They shrug off objections with a nonchalant national stereotyping: 'But aren't *all* Italians like that?'[29]

How far Italian attitudes (though not British) have changed can be gauged by comparing the present situation with that of thirteen years previously, when Italy held the European Presidency from July to December 1990. Then Giulio Andreotti was the Italian premier, Helmut Kohl the German Chancellor and François Mitterrand the French President. Together they spun a Roman web into which Mrs. Thatcher fell, and which was eventually to cost her job as Prime Minister. Andreotti and Thatcher, Italy and Britain were far apart in how they viewed politics, in their conception of national interest, and in their view of the future of the European Union. That is no longer necessarily the case.

A strategy such as the one briefly outlined above has a coherence which commands respect, if not necessarily consent. No such thing can be said about Berlusconi's first days as President of the Council of Europe, a post Italy has held from July to December of 2003. On 2 July he made his opening speech to the European parliament.

29 See Charlemagne, 'Burlesquoni', *The Economist*, 12 July 2003.

It was an acceptable and careful affair, but afterwards the Eurode-
puties began to question him. Martin Schulz, the Vice President of
the German social democrats in the parliament, asked him to explain
why Italy was blocking the idea of a European arrest warrant for
crimes such as corruption, why it had introduced the new law on
international rogatories, and why the request of the Spanish magistrate Garzón to remove Berlusconi's and Dell'Utri's European parliamentary immunity had not reached the Assembly. It was provocative but legitimate stuff, and an experienced politician would have
parried it without difficulty. Not Berlusconi. With an acutely embar-
rassed Giancarlo Fini sitting next to him, Berlusconi replied that a
producer he knew was in Italy making a film about the Nazi concentration camps: 'I shall recommend you, Signor Schulz, for the role
of camp guard'. According to the *Corriere della Sera*'s correspondent,
Berlusconi's words, simultaneously translated, were greeted by the
Assembly with 'an unbelieving ooohhh of protest'.[30] The uproar in
the international press, including its liberal and conservative sections,
was immense.[31] Berlusconi apologised, but then denied that he had
ever done so. Never had his limitations been so glaringly apparent.

A few days later, a European opinion poll revealed the damage
done. Asked which European premier could most be trusted, other
than their own, the German sample replied with 51 percent for Chirac,
19 percent for Blair, 8 percent for Aznar and only 2 percent for

---

30 Claudio Lindner, 'Scontro all'esordio europeo di Berlusconi', *Corriere della Sera*, 3
July 2003. The lunchtime edition of the news on RAI 1 offered so heavily edited a version
of what had happened that Ernesto Galli Della Loggia, a well-known editorialist on the
Corriere della Sera not known for his radical views, denounced it for being 'grotesquely
incomplete and manipulatory'; 'Un pessimo inizio', ivi, 3 July.

31 Berlusconi was heavily condemned in both the Israeli and the German press. The
cartoonist Altan (*la Repubblica*, 3 July 2003) depicted a grim-faced Italian girl on the beach.
The caption read: 'There are still six months to go before the beginning of the Irish
Presidency of the European Union'.

Berlusconi; the French with 54 percent for Schroeder, 37 percent for Blair, 23 percent for Aznar and 11 percent for Berlusconi; the Spanish with 51 percent for Chirac, 50 percent for Schroeder, 48 percent for Blair and 17 percent for Berlusconi; and finally the British, no lovers of Continental politicians, with 19 percent for Schroeder, 16 percent for Aznar, 15 percent for Chirac and just 7 percent for Berlusconi.[32] However, such widespread discrediting has not been translated into any concerted European action. The politicians of the European Union, even those politically opposed to Berlusconi, seem content to turn a blind eye. The Union appears incapable of dealing with the radical undermining of democracy in one of its founder states.[33]

5. History and Culture

A final word must be added concerning the government's attitude to the past, and to Italy's very considerable cultural heritage. Italy must be amongst the most historically sensitive countries in the world. The past matters here, sometimes very much. During the Berlusconi government, for obvious reasons, it is Fascism that has been a particularly contested historical terrain. Ever since the publication between 1965 and 1997 of Renzo De Felice's monumental biography of Mussolini, broadly empathetic towards Il Duce, a process of re-evaluation of the regime and its leader has been under way. In many ways revisionism of this sort must be considered as highly positive,

32 Marco Damiliano, 'Il più bocciato dagli europei', *L'Espresso*, 17 July 2003, pp. 28–32.

33 The experience of the Haider affair seems to have condemned the Union to paralysis. See M. Merlingen et al., 'The right and the righteous? European norms, domestic politics and the sanctions against Austria', *Journal of Common Market Studies*, vol. 39 (2001), no. 1, pp. 59–77.

because it has caused historians to argue over and redefine views of Fascism that had become tired and ritualistic.

However, the political use made of this debate has been highly instrumental. The official rhetoric of the centre-right has maintained that Fascism was not such a bad thing after all, that Mussolini was led astray by Hitler, and that only after 1938, with the introduction of the infamous anti-Semitic laws, did the regime go off the rails. Such attitudes can be traced back at least to 1994, when Gianfranco Fini made his already-mentioned statement about Mussolini being the greatest statesman of the twentieth century. In those same days Irene Pivetti, the League's young and controversial choice as Speaker of the House of Deputies, declared how well women had been treated under Fascism.[34]

The rhetorical strategy behind such declarations always follows the same pattern. The statement is first made in brutal and uncompromising fashion. Uproar follows. Depending upon the volume of protest, a partial retraction or 'clarification' is then forthcoming. But the damage has been done, and as the wily Christian Democrat Giulio Andreotti once said: 'A "retraction" always means that a piece of infomation has been communicated twice'.[35]

The most recent incident in this long offensive was Berlusconi's interview with Boris Johnson and Nicholas Farrell of *The Spectator*, published in two instalments on 6 and 13 September 2003. 'Mussolini', said Berlusconi, 'did not murder anyone'. His was a 'benign dictatorship' and instead of imprisoning his opponents he 'sent people on holiday', to islands such as Ponza and Ventotene.[36] All these statements are obviously false. To rebut only the most serious, Fascist thugs killed many a trade unionist between 1920 and 1922, Il Duce took direct responsibility for the abduction and killing of the Socialist

34 Barabara Palombelli, 'E venne Santa Irene . . .', *la Repubblica*, 23 April 1994.
35 Ibid.
36 Nicholas Farrell, 'Diary', *The Spectator*, 13 September 2003.

deputy Giacomo Matteotti in 1924, and his policies lead directly to tens of thousands of deaths between 1936 and 1945 – Abyssinian, Spanish, British, American, Italian, Greek, Albanian and so on. Even the Italian right-wing press complained about the wanton lies of this interview. Berlusconi's 'clarification' followed: 'I did not intend to revalue Mussolini but simply, as an Italian, I did not accept the comparison [made by the interviewer] between my country and the dictatorship of Saddam Hussein, which provoked millions of deaths'.[37]

In the decade that has intervened between Fini's statement of 1994 and Berlusconi's of 2003, many centre-right local governments have taken the opportunity to rehabilitate 'good' Fascists.[38] Sadly, the ambiguities of the centre-left have contributed to these revisionist trends. After its victory in 1996, much of the coalition decided to speak the language of 'national reconciliation'. It was time, so it was said, for bygones to be bygones. The young men who had fought for the Republic of Salò (Mussolini's puppet Republic of 1943–45) and those who had fought in the Resistance were to be equally respected, for they had been motivated by patriotic sentiments. In 1995, the centre-left mayor of Rome, Francesco Rutelli, had proposed naming a square after Giuseppe Bottai, one of the Fascist regime's more 'liberal' leaders. It was only after widespread protests, and the reminder of Bottai's anti-Semitism, that Rutelli climbed down.[39]

37 Amedeo La Mattina, 'Scontro per una frase di Berlusconi su Mussolini', *La Stampa*, 12 September 2003. The specific context in the interview was instead the following: 'While discussing Iraq, Berlusconi said, "I understand the difficulties in teaching democracy to a people who for nearly forty years have known only dictatorship". To which I said, in a jocular way, "Like Italy at the fall of fascism". He replied, "That was a much more benign dictatorship – Mussolini did not murder anyone."'

38 Public buildings have been renamed in memory of one of the national secretaries of Mussolini's Fascist party, Adelchi Serena, and at Bari the seafront promenade now bears the name of the old Fascist mayor, Araldo di Crollalanza; Gianpasquale Santomassimo, 'Il rapporto con il passato', in Id. (ed.), *La notte della democrazia italiana*, p. 161.

39 Ibid., pp. 160–62.

The Berlusconi government has now decided to take history in hand. There is to be a new public holiday, the Day of Liberty, 9 November, which will celebrate the knocking down of the Berlin Wall.[40] Italian school textbooks are to be rewritten, on the grounds that they are too left-wing. Henceforth they are to follow 'objective criteria which respect historical truth'.[41] Here is a short extract from one of the first products of this new pursuit of objectivity. It is aimed at fourteen-year-olds and refers to the first decades of Italian unity after 1870:

> The men of the Right were aristocrats and great landowners. They entered politics with the sole intention of serving the State, not to enrich themselves or climb up the social ladder. Furthermore, they administered the finances of the State with the same attention and parsimony with which they cared for their own patrimonies. The men of the Left, on the other hand, are [note change of tense] professionals, entrepreneurs and lawyers, ready to further their careers in any way. Sometimes, they sacrifice the good of the Nation to their own interests. The great difference between the governments of the Right and those of the Left consists above all in their diverse moral and political attitudes.[42]

~

As for Italy's immense cultural heritage, the government's measures to privatise its administration and facilitate the selling-off of some

40 www.forza-italia.it, November 2003. The first signature on the bill was that of the Forza Italia senator Sergio Travaglia.

41 Gabriele Turi, 'Una storia italiana', *Passato e Presente*, vol. 21 (2003), no. 59, pp. 89–98.

42 Federica Bellesini, *I nuovi sentieri della Storia. Il Novecento*, Novara 2003, p. 34. I must thank a colleague from the State University of Milan, whose daughter had to use this book in class, for the above information.

parts of it have aroused widespread international protest. In December 2001, the directors of the United States' principal museums, together with thirty-three of their counterparts from all over the world, signed a petition against the Italian government's plans. Berlusconi and his Treasury Minister, Tremonti, went ahead all the same, passing a new law in June 2002. In it provision has been made for the creation of two limited companies, one to manage the State's patrimony and the other its infrastructures. Both are to benefit from considerable deregulation, aimed at reducing the impact of a formidable legal and technical apparatus, developed over a long period of time, and dedicated to both protection and conservation. The principal aims of the government seem clear enough: more efficient administration, less restrictive laws, and the possibility of opening up for private sale parts of Italy's *beni culturali*, an operation certain to bolster the ailing finances of the State.

The law of June 2002 takes us back to the heart of Berlusconi's overall project, for at stake here are two very different conceptions of patrimony. The first is that of the centre-right government, which privileges the private over the public, the flexible over the inflexible, and immediate cash flows over long-term interests. It is convinced that individual fruition and opportunity are the best guarantors of collective interest. The second view of patrimony, a public one, is well explained by Salvatore Settis, the Director of one of Italy's most prestigious academic institutions, the Scuola Normale at Pisa:

It is the opposite of proprietary individualism, which emphasizes exclusive rights of use and disposal. Instead, its principal references are to collective values, to social links and responsibilities. Only with reference to a common patrimony of culture and memory can these take the form of a pact of citizenship. . . . It is thanks to this conception, which implies a strong and well-directed action on the part of the State, that Siena is still recognisably a mediaeval city, that Venice has no skyscrapers, that the Leaning Tower of Pisa, which does not belong to the State, has not been abandoned to its destiny but 'straightened up' at the state's expense.[43]

A centuries' old tradition of public action and expertise, deeply rooted in territorial terms, now risks being starved of funds, as is the case in so many parts of the Italian State.

Berlusconi's Culture Minister, Giuliano Urbani, insists that such fears are ill-founded. What the government wishes to sell are not cultural treasures, but ex-barracks fallen into disuse, thousands of buildings which have been abandoned or are badly used, and so on. The funds will then be directed back into cultural conservation.[44] But the terms of the government's law are much wider than this, leaving ample room for abuse. Nor, as we have seen, can any reassurance be drawn from the government's terrible record for granting remissions, amnesties and dispensations to cover previous abusive construction of private houses, and damage to the landscape and environment. In all these areas, an individualist concept of patrimonial power has been revealed in transparent form, with grave implications for the democratic tradition in Italy.

6. Conclusions

In a relaxed moment at the beginning of June 2002, Berlusconi explained to Italian journalists his essentially paternal functions as head of the government. From Cabinet, parliament and society came many

43 Salvatore Settis, *Italia S.p.a.*, Turin 2003, pp. 25 and 88.
44 Giuliano Urbani, '"Silenzio-assenso? Nessun rischio. Noi non svendiamo il patrimonio"', *Corriere della Sera*, 3 December 2003.

requests for governmental expenditure, 'just as a wife asks for a new
boiler after the electrician has been called too many times, a daughter
for the money to enrol on an English language course, a son to change
the family car. But we, just like a father, must discriminate with good
sense between the various requests'.[45] Things have not gone at all like
this.

The poor showing of the Berlusconi government lends itself to
various explanations. One is that 'overpromising', which, as Mény
and Surel have suggested, is a typical feature of modern populism. In
Berlusconi's case the promises, as we have seen, were solemn and
staged on television. Very few of them have so far been kept. Another
explanation, much propagated by the veteran political commentator
Giancarlo Pansa, concentrates on the quality of Berlusconi's team. His
project may be ambitious, but the human capital employed on it is
for the most part mediocre and inexperienced. A third, already
mentioned, is that the downturn in the economy has rendered
fulfilment very much more difficult.

All these reasons have much to recommend them, but need to be
placed in the wider context of the tensions that exist between the
various parts – patrimonial, populist, neoliberal – of Berlusconi's
project. The primacy of his own interests, their overspilling into the
public sphere, and their necessary defence in tricky and frankly
suspect circumstances, have taken their toll. Although the Italians
have not shown a particular sensibility to questions such as the conflict
of interests and the autonomy of the judiciary, by May 2003 some 59
percent of them thought that if Berlusconi was found guilty of
corrupting judges in the SME case, even just at the first level, he
should resign.[46] For a long time Berlusconi played on the fact that his

45 R.de Gennaro, 'Berlusconi felice', *la Repubblica*, 1 June 2002.
46 F.Bordignon, 'Gli italiani bocciano l'immunità', *la Repubblica*, 17 May 2003.

own patrimonial ambitions not only did not damage his populist appeal but enhanced it. There are signs, evident if not conclusive, that these two elements have entered into conflict with each other.

Secondly, the neoliberalism of some of his most active ministers, like Letizia Moratti, with their insistence on privatisation and a highly flexible labour market, and a corresponding weakening of worker and citizen rights, is anathema to a populist project that seeks to reassure and integrate, not atomise and divide. The economic downturn, with its redundancies and increasing sense of risk, has obviously heightened such a contradiction. Neoliberalism had great purchase and fascination at its inception more than twenty years ago. The 'invisible hand' of the market seemed to offer infinite possibilities for acquisition and upward mobility to individuals and their families. A late and tired version, in very different global circumstances, does not appear to possess such alchemic powers. The major preoccupation of the Italians, revealed by all the opinion polls, is the finding and keeping of work. At a time of economic downturn, neoliberal cutbacks of state expenditure offer very little reassurance in this respect. Nor does the prospect of privatising the administration of Italy's cultural heritage and selling off parts of it do anything to reassure educated public opinion.

A final contradiction exists in the tension between the rhetoric of a free-market philosophy, oft-proclaimed, and the reality of a personalistic and sometimes monopolistic control of resources and opportunities, as in the field of communications. Very recently a group of businessmen from the north-east of the country, amongst whom was Luciano Benetton, wrote to the Prime Minister. They complained bitterly that they were being prevented from investing in southern regions where the House of Liberties holds political power. 'Too often', wrote the industrialists, 'local exponents of your coalition behave as if the contract with the Italians which you signed is simply a question that regards your own person'.[47] Here it is Berlusconi's patrimonialism, not his populism, which enters into conflict with a free-market philosophy. All the signs point to this conflict deepening with the new law on Telecommunications, which has once again, as in 1990, been written in Berlusconi's image. Mediaset is set to retain its three national commercial channels transmitting terrestrially, whereas the Constitutional Court has explicitly forbidden one proprietor from having more than two such channels, and has ordered Rete 4 to transfer to cable or satellite.

Silvio Berlusconi has not performed well to date, and recent events have greatly complicated his project. On no account, though, should he be underestimated. He has no intention of resigning and has always shown very considerable reserves of energy and determination in times of difficulty. Although the opinion polls are now unfavourable to him, more than 40 percent of Italians are still firmly on his side, a tribute to the enduring permeative powers of his overall project, and to the chords it strikes in Italian society.

47 The letter was published as a paid insert in *Corriere della Sera*, 5 February 2003.

7. RESISTANCES

1. Institutions

Within the State, it has been the judiciary that has been most under attack. The House of Liberties' lack of a sense of limits and its anthropological need to be free from restraint have made this attack inevitable, even if its leader had not been personally involved in a number of trials. For the most part, the judiciary has responded with tenacity and determination. Historically, they have been far from a united group, riven rather by political influence and faction fighting. Berlusconi has forced a cohesion upon them which would have been unthinkable in other circumstances.

In many ways the opening of the juridical year (an event of pomp and circumstance in the Italian institutional calendar) on 12 January 2002 was a major point of departure. A significant number of magistrates and judges – the two are organically connected in Italy by forming part of the same career structure – deserted the opening ceremonies in their respective cities, leaving black togas draped symbolically across abandoned seats. Francesco Saverio Borrelli made a last speech before retirement. He invited the judiciary to 'resist, resist, resist', as general Cadorna had invited the Italian army to do on the line of the Piave during the First World War, in the critical weeks of October and November 1917, when the Austrians seemed poised to break through to the Po plain. It was from Borrelli's words that many of the subsequent actions in civil society took their cue. In June 2002, and again in November 2003, the magistrates organised highly successful one-day strikes, and Berlusconi's continuing verbal assault on the judiciary ('they are nothing but a self-interested corporation', 'the judges are anthropologically different from the rest of the population', 'you'd have to be mad to be a magistrate') led to a further closing of the ranks.

However, no one should bet on the judiciary seeing off the challenge. A Minister of Justice hell-bent on reform, with an ample parliamentary majority behind him and more than two years of the legislature ahead, cannot easily be stopped. Already, the composition of the Higher Council of the Magistracy has been changed, with more representation being given to political appointees. Furthermore, it is not clear what support can be mustered from other parts of the State apparatus. If we return for a moment to the question of what antibodies democratic states offer in the face of newly personalised power, then the case of Italy is not a comforting one. The lack of a developed ethos of public service in many parts of the administration, the uncertainty of the rule of law, the tradition of *trasformismo*, that is the willingness of politicians and administrators to abandon long-stated views and adapt their principles to changed political circumstances, all of these argue against a protracted and coherent institutional resistance to Berlusconi's project.

The opposition that will come from within the State is of a different quality. In the Italian Republic the passing of legislation and its subsequent implementation is frequently a complicated and accident-laden sequence of events. Pushing reform through, of whatever sort, is uphill work. The slowness of parliamentary procedures, the absence of administrative cooperation and efficiency, the recourse to administrative law, are only some of the mechanisms that can undermine a government's programme. Berlusconi and his colleagues have already felt the negative effects of these procedural *longueurs*. If it is true that reorganisation of the central State in July 1999 led to an improvement in its functioning, it is also true that the formalism of Italian administrative culture and its demotivated civil servants are a great obstacle to efficient government.[1]

There is another institutional resistance, subtle and not to be underestimated. Luigi Bobbio has referred recently to the 'disassociation' that exists in Italy between two different ways of approaching government, and indeed between two different administrative worlds. The first, very much in the Berlusconi mould, speaks the rhetoric of decisiveness. It combines the business culture of Forza Italia with the lingering authoritarianism of the National Alliance. Decisions are there to be taken, swiftly, with no nonsense, using the power conferred by a strong parliamentary majority. This first world believes in the necessary tyranny of the majority and zero sum games. It is highly visible – on television, in the newspapers, on the talk shows. The second world, by contrast, is opaque, almost underground. It speaks the rhetoric of agreement. It believes in decision-making as an inclusive, not exclusive process, painstaking and time-consuming. Its mode of action corresponds not only to the reality of much of Italy's local government, but to that of the European Union. Even if essentially passive, this second world acts as a powerful braking mechanism on the headlong rush of the first.[2]

~

1 Mark Donovan, 'Berlusconi, strong government and the Italian state', *Journal of Modern Italian Studies*, vol. VIII (2003), no. 2, pp. 231–48; for a less optimistic view, Sabino Cassese, 'Il sistema amministrativo italiano, ovvero l'arte di arrangiarsi', in S.Cassese and C.Franchini (eds), *L'amministrazione pubblica italiana*, Bologna 1994, pp. 13–21.

2 Luigi Bobbio, 'La disassociazione italiana', article in the course of publication.

Turning away from structures to individual agency, the position of the President of the Republic is a particularly delicate and important one. The President has limited powers of intervention, but is expected to set the moral and political tone for the country. His is the New Year's message to the Italians, his the task of almost daily speech-making at official events. At the time of the Clean Hands campaign in the early 1990s, it was the President of the Republic, the ex-Christian Democrat Oscar Luigi Scalfaro, who gave explicit backing to the anti-corruption offensive of the reforming minority of magistrates.

The present incumbent at the Quirinale palace, the widely respected former Governor of the Bank of Italy and ex-Prime Minister, Carlo Azeglio Ciampi, has chosen a much more cautious line. He has made it clear that the centre-right's parliamentary majority gives it the full right to govern, but at the same time he has tried to exercise some control over its actions. Consequently, he has worked behind the scenes, proposing and modifying as the case arises. He urged, as we have noted, the appointment of Renato Ruggiero upon a reluctant Berlusconi, and insisted on the modifying of a crucial phrase in the Cirami law, thus giving the Corte di Cassazione more space to manoeuvre. His attempted bi-partisan policies have won the appreciation of most of the government (with the exception of the Northern League), and most of the opposition. His popularity ratings are higher than those of any other figure in the country.

Yet more than once ostensible control has bordered on complicity. The President of the Republic has never made explicit the corrosive effects of the government's actions upon Italian democracy. Two factors play their part here. One is the nature of the Presidency itself. The Quirinale — as the bizarre behaviour of more than one of its occupants has taught us in the past — is not a good place from which to understand Italian history or society. Both its isolation and its endless agenda of formal appointments, with the constant presence there of 'official' Italy, take their toll. Secondly, Ciampi is more than eighty years old. He is as astute as ever, but age appears to have accentuated those predilections for caution and compromise that have always been a strong element of his character. His untiring patriotic propaganda, with its hoped-for vision of a nation united by its virtues (and its national anthem), rather than divided by its vices, is highly revealing in this regard. The unity of a democratic community is certainly a precious good, but it has to be founded on a certain minimum number of non-negotiable bases.

In this regard, Ciampi's responsibility for the immunity law which was passed by parliament in June 2003, and which effectively allowed Berlusconi to escape judicial judgement, is a very grave one. It was Ciampi who initiated a process of what he called 'moral suasion' to convince all parties that this was the proper solution to the problem. Italy was just about to take over the presidency of the European Union. To risk having an Italian president convicted of corrupting judges right in the middle of his six-month tenure was for Ciampi a quite unacceptable scenario. Rather, the country had to maintain its 'bella figura'. Such a line of argument was deeply flawed on at least two counts. It prevented justice from being seen to be done, thus undermining fatally ten years of the magistrates' work in Milan; and it did not contribute an inch to the creation of a 'bella figura', for this last-minute immunity law was greeted with derision by most of European public opinion. When Ciampi went to Berlin on 26 June 2003 to reopen the Italian embassy and to speak at the Humboldt University, a young Italian Ph.D. student, Elena Paba, got to her feet and asked the President: 'Why, before coming here, did you sign the immunity law?' Her question was greeted with prolonged applause by German students and professors.[3]

~

As for the parliamentary opposition of the Olive Tree coalition, it has been uncertain from the start, caught between its wish to deny that anything significant was happening, and the daily and unmistakable evidence that something was. For seven months, from June 2001 to January 2002, the opposition remained in a coma. During this time its prevailing view was that the House of Liberties represented no fundamental threat, and in many ways would do the same thing as the centre-left had done, only with less competence. As has already been noted, no serious analysis of Berlusconi's project emerged from its ranks, still less a critique of its own years in government.

The behaviour of the major centre-left parties in this period brings to mind the unsparing analysis which Juan Linz made of those democratic forces in the first half of the twentieth century which failed to prevent the destruction of democracy in many parts of Europe. Linz uses the expression 'semiloyal' to describe them. Although such parties would have been outraged at the idea of being considered 'semiloyal' to democracy, their actions belied their words. Time and again, they failed to see the danger looming on the horizon, they were prepared to enter into secret negotiations, they were willing to 'encourage, tolerate, cover up, treat leniently, excuse or justify' actions which demanded quite other reactions.[4] The situation in Italy today, as I have made quite clear, is not that of eighty years ago. Yet it is still possible to discern some of the same patterns of uncertainty,

3 Vincenzo Vasile, 'L'Europa non si fida, Ciampi ne fa le spese', *l'Unità*, 27 June 2003. See also above, p. 146, n. 21.

4 Juan J. Linz, 'Crisis, breakdown, and reequilibration', in Id. and Alfred Stepan (eds), *The Breakdown of Democratic Regimes*, Baltimore and London 1978, p. 32.

opportunism and accommodation. Time and again these are dressed up as 'a sense of responsibility', but they are nothing of the sort.

In the face of what is undoubtedly an extraordinary threat, the Olive Tree coalition seems incapable of transforming the tired and partially discredited nature of its politics. The coalition's constituent parts and leaders jockey endlessly for position. Their politics remain extraordinarily self-referential, confined almost entirely to the parliamentary palace of Montecitorio. At a local level, as one sober critique put it in April 2002:

> The rhythms, rituals and lexicon of [left-wing] politics today leave much to be desired. Meetings are interminable and badly organised, spoken interventions are too long, rhetoric too often prevails over reason, aspiring leaders over the less ambitious, men over women. Meetings, anyway, are often the exclusive political activity of those who organise them. We could say, provocatively, that it seems as if politics exists for meetings, not meetings for politics. To change a political culture of this sort is a long-term, even Utopian project.[5]

As for Rifondazione Comunista, it suffers from many of the same faults. Sealed up in a ghetto of its own making, too often convinced of the natural superiority of its own politics, it has been too sectarian and too small to make much difference one way or another.

2. Society

From January 2002 onwards, this depressing picture was radically transformed by a wave of protest, as vast as it was unexpected,

---

5 'Documento presentato all'Assemblea Costituente del Laboratorio per la Democrazia di Firenze', 6 April 2002.

which swept through many parts of Italian civil society.[6] Although the actors in this protest often overlapped and collaborated one with another, it is possible to discern three distinct strands: the first of these was a revitalised trade union movement, centred upon the CGIL and its then leader Sergio Cofferati. It was the CGIL which organised in March 2002 what became the largest demonstration in the history of the Republic, with between two and three million people from every part of the peninsula gathered in Rome, in and around the Circo Massimo. The protest was against the government's proposed abolition of article 18 of the Workers' Statute of 1972, which prevents employers from sacking workers 'without just cause'.

The second strand was a largely middle-class movement, motivated primarily but not exclusively by questions of justice and pluralism of information. Here too the protest received its consecration in the form of an extraordinary demonstration, this time in Piazza San Giovanni in Rome on 14 September 2002. Born of the outrage felt at the proposed Cirami law, the demonstration gathered more than 800,000 people, in and around Rome's largest piazza. It was self-financed, without the presence or aid of the centre-left parties. Nanni Moretti, one of Italy's most famous film directors, made the opening speech; the ninety-one-year-old former trade union leader, Vittorio Foa, one of the concluding ones.

The final strand is that of the new global movement, drawing its sustenance above all from the generation now aged between eighteen and twenty-five, loosely federated in the Social Forums of all Italy's major cities. Italy's Social Forums are the strongest and most active in Europe, and it was in recognition of this fact that the first European

6 For a good introduction to that moment, see the collection of articles in *MicroMega*, no. 2, 2002, with the general title *La primavera dei movimenti*. See also Edoardo Ferrario, 'Cronologia dei girotondi', ivi, 2003, no. 2.

Social Forum was held in Florence in November of 2002. The event, as has already been mentioned, led to the outbreak of mass hysteria in the media and parliament. Some 40,000 people participated from all over Europe, and the Forum came to an end with another massive and peaceful demonstration, against the imminent threat of war in Iraq. Nearly one million people took part. On 15 February 2003, concurrent with other peace demonstrations worldwide, between two and three million people once again marched through Rome.

This sequence of events, which made 2002 one of the most remarkable years in recent Italian history, lends itself to a number of comments. The first concerns numbers. At a time when mainstream sociological comment was insistent upon the essential and indeed 'permanent' apathy of contemporary societies, the numbers of people taking part in the Italian protests exceeded not only the wildest hopes of their organisers, but are comparable to those involved in Italy's previous mass protests, even during the 'Hot Autumn' of workers' struggles in 1969–70.

Another striking feature was the massive presence of educated middle-class protesters, enraged by Berlusconi's actions, but also increasingly impatient with the quality and leadership of the centre-left coalition. It was a Florentine university professor, Francesco 'Pancho' Pardi, a geographer, who denounced the Olive Tree leaders in Rome's Piazza Navona on 2 February 2002 for their mistakes in government and insipid opposition. When the same leaders went on with their prepared speeches as if he had never spoken, Nanni Moretti got up on the podium to make a memorable short speech, which concluded with the words: 'With this lot in charge we shall never win an election again'.[7] From that moment onwards, left-wing politics in Italy were not to be the same.

7 Concetta De Gregorio, 'L'ultimo urlo di Nanni', la Repubblica, 3 February 2002.

The Italian middle classes had long been denounced for their egoism and indifference. However, the monotony and predictability of such comments masked the emergence of a 'reflexive' middle class, concentrated for the most part amongst teachers, public sector technicians and management, educated women who have recently entered the labour market, the lower ranks of the professions, students and some of those who work in the media and in information technology. These members of the middle class looked critically upon Italy's model of modernity, as well as the role ascribed to them within it.[8] They insisted instead, and with increasing vehemence, not only on the defence of democracy against the Berlusconi government, but also on its profound renewal. Throughout 2002 many of them took as their themes not just the autonomy of the judiciary and pluralism of information, but also deliberative democracy, fair trade and responsible consumption, immigrant rights, a critique of the narcissism and careerism of much of the political class of the centre-left. Their protests took a number of forms: the most famous was that of the *girotondo*, in which demonstrators hold hands in a series of moving concentric circles to surround a public building or other objective. Law courts, television studios, other public buildings which needed to be symbolically protected, became the sites for such demonstrations. Other forms of organisation included the founding of associations, networks and 'Laboratories for Democracy', of which the Florentine was the first and most influential. The eruption of this new, autonomous middle-

8 For further discussion of this theme and some European comparisons, P. Ginsborg, *Italy and its Discontents*, pp. 42–4; Id., Perry Anderson, John Foot and Simon Parker, 'Italy in the present time: a roundtable discussion', *Modern Italy*, vol. 5 (2000), no. 2, pp. 175–91; Bernard Cassen, 'Inventing ATTAC', *New Left Review*, New Series, 2003, no. 19, p. 46. On a theoretical level, see the intense debate in U.Beck, A.Giddens, S.Lash, *Reflexive Modernisation: Politics, Tradition and Aesthetics in Modern Social Order*, Cambridge 1994.

class protest in Italian society attracted the attention of a number of foreign observers.[9]

We must be careful, in spite of the often innovatory aspects of the various parts of the protests of 2002, not to exaggerate their strength. The movement is quite patchy, with some parts of the country moving hardly at all. If Florence and Tuscany have formed an epicentre, Bologna and Emilia-Romagna have been less active than might have been expected. Northern cities, once historic sites of left-wing elaboration and experiment, such as Turin, hardly stirred. In the South there has been some activity in Naples and Palermo, but vast parts of the southern provinces, as has so often happened in the past, have only been touched marginally. The trade union component of the movement has had its own difficulties, because the more moderate unions, the CISL and UIL, refused to follow the lead of the CGIL in 2002. That unity of the working-class movement, which was one of the most sought-after objectives of the Italian Left, and one of the most positive outcomes of the struggles of the 1960s and 1970s, was absent throughout that year. The activism of the new global movement, which through the city Social Forums has shown a remarkable capacity for coordinating very disparate groups (Catholic, revolutionary socialist, trade union, environmentalist, etc.), continues unabated, though it has been difficult to maintain momentum after the European Social Forum in Florence. The year 2003 was a much quieter year than the previous one. When the '*girotondini*' tried to organise mass protests against the immunity law of June 2003, they met with lukewarm responses practically everywhere.[10]

The wave of protests, involving overlapping groups of young people, trade unionists, and 'reflexive' middle class, has not found a

9 See, for instance, R.Arens, 'Italiens neue Apo' and 'Italiens Mitte bewegt sich doch', *Frankfurter Rundschau*, 6 March 2002.

10 Vladimiro Polchi, 'Girotondi, appello a Ciampi', *la Repubblica*, 19 June 2002.

satisfactory political outlet. The Left Democrats have spent the last year organising debates about the relationship between the movement and the parties, without changing in any significant way their politics or mode of behaviour. Calls for primaries to decide party candidatures have been met with suspicion. Massimo D'Alema has consistently adopted a hostile and arrogant attitude towards the protests; many thousands of left-democrat municipal, provincial and regional administrators, fearing their careers are at stake, are firmly behind him. The internal opposition within the party is too weak to claim the leadership. As for Rifondazione Comunista, it commands the enthusiastic support of part of the new global movement, but little else. Its leader, Fausto Bertinotti, did not waste a moment in condemning the new middle-class protests as 'petty-bourgeois', and subordinate in any case to the 'movement of movements'. Dogma dies hard.

At the beginning of 2003, the most popular figure on the Left was undoubtedly Sergio Cofferati, who had left the CGIL at the end of his period of service as general secretary. He appeared at the time to offer the possibility of an alternative leadership, attentive and respectful of all parts of Italian civil society, and insistent upon the need to innovate both in method and in programme. However, he faltered during the year, uncertain of the real force of the movements of 2002, unwilling to break with the Left Democrat leadership, and cleverly undermined by Fausto Bertinotti, who feared his leadership. By the autumn of 2003 he had decided to fall back on being the Olive Tree candidate for Mayor of Bologna. It was a decision that was greeted with dismay by his many supporters in civil society.

The Italian Left and the Olive Tree coalition thus remain uncertain and fissiparous, an inadequate political representation of the forces which mobilised during 2002. The impelling need to unite in order to defeat Berlusconi's coalition will undoubtedly generate some centripetal movement, and the prospect of Romano Prodi's leadership, once he returns from Brussels in the autumn of 2004, is one that commands very wide support. Yet centrifugal and warring forces remain insidious and powerful. History is, unfortunately, on their side. Exceptional capacities of pragmatism and idealism, of ability to compromise as well as to mobilise, will be needed in the coming months. So far, they have not been that much in evidence.

POSTSCRIPT

It is 24 January 2004. Silvio Berlusconi is celebrating the tenth anniversary of his famous decision to enter politics. He has been mysteriously absent from Rome for more than twenty days, a disappearance that has given rise to more than one rumour. Suddenly, all is revealed. He has had a face-lift over Christmas. Here he is again, beaming happily to his six thousand delirious admirers crammed into the great Congress hall of the Roman suburb of EUR, built at the time of Fascism. The bags under his eyes have diminished in size, the face has been drawn expertly upwards. The women of Forza Italia are ecstatic: 'He looks better than a twenty-year-old'; 'he's shown once again, if you'll pardon the expression, what a pair of balls he's got'; 'for me he's a genius'; 'I wish I'd had his plastic surgeon'. The tall and elegant Stefania Prestigiacomo, Minister of Equal Opportunities and Mistress of Ceremonies for the afternoon, insists that a face-lift is nothing to be ashamed of: 'It's not the first time that a male politician has had one, but it's the first time that one of them has said so. Silvio simply has more courage than all the others'.[1] The widespread discussion of Berlusconi's face-lift serves as a remarkable indicator of shifting priorities in Italian public life, of the vital importance that appearance and image have assumed in a screen-dominated personality culture.

1 Luca Telese, 'E le signore benedicono il lifting', *Il Giornale*, 25 January 2004.

Berlusconi makes a speech which lasts an hour and a half. He returns once again to his view of liberty: 'For us liberty is an individual right which precedes society and precedes the State. The State exists in order to protect the liberty of every one, but it is not the fount of liberty for all.' When the Left had been in power, the State had been too invasive, the unions had too much influence, the institutions of the country had been infiltrated by left-wing placemen. 'The Communists', he intones 'tried having a face-lift, in order to hide their real identity, but theirs failed.' Pursuing for a moment the logic of this argument, it is not quite clear what Berlusconi's own face-lift has successfully concealed.

The political culture of Forza Italia, Berlusconi continues, is liberal, Catholic, social and popular, but he cannot resist making reference to Fascism as well: 'Better Fascism', he proclaims to resounding applause, 'than the bureaucratic tyranny of the judiciary.' He lists the achievements of his government: the increase of the minimum pension, 450,000 people who have emerged from poverty, 750,000 new jobs, the abolition of the inheritance tax, an education reform which has 'given our children the posibility of a truly formative education, adapted to modern life'. The speech finishes on a favourite theme, and in upbeat style: 'We have in mind a country in which every young person has faith in himself, in his own possibility of making a success of his life, of not having the door closed in his face when he asks for a loan to invest in a house or a business. . . . We have in mind a country where truth prevails over lies, a country where concrete action takes the place of idle chatter, a country above all where love triumphs over hate.'[2]

~

2 Silvio Berlusconi, 'Discorso del 24 gennaio 2004', ibid. For other accounts and details, including the reading of the 'Secular Credo' of the party, a compilation of

Ten years in the life of party, and of a leader, are worth celebrating, but the months go by and the situation of the Berlusconi government gets no better. No triumph greeted the end of the Italian presidency of the European Union, and no agreement was reached over the system of voting to be enshrined in the new European Constitution. Berlusconi's own small-scale presence on the international scene has been confirmed by this failure. At home, nothing has improved. The cost of living remains unacceptably high, and all the statistics show how real wages have been eroded over the past two years. The spectacular failure of one of the few Italian transnational companies, Parmalat, has done nothing for business confidence. Thousands of small investors have lost their savings. As a result, we have been treated to the odd spectacle of those same centre-right politicians who abolished the severe laws on accounting fraud now calling for more rigorous control of business accounting and financial speculation. Berlusconi's Treasury Minister, Giulio Tremonti, has used the occasion to launch an attack upon the Bank of Italy, complaining that the Bank should have warned investors in time. His attack is reminiscent of that launched by the centre-right against the Bank in 1994, and the long-term objective is the same: to reduce the autonomy of one of Italy's most prestigious institutions, and if possible to replace its Governor.[3]

Berlusconi's battle for overall control has received two recent setbacks in the areas closest to his heart and to his interests: his own fate in the law courts, and the further de-regulation of Italy's mass media. On the judicial front, in November 2003, his lawyer friend

---

quotations from the Great Man, and the role of Don Baget Bozzo in the ceremony, see Gian Antonio Stella, 'La rivelazione alla platea: ci spinse lo Spirito Santo', *Corriere della Sera*, 25 January 2004; Concita De Gregorio, 'La messa cantata di Silvio con gli anatemi di don Gianni', *la Repubblica*, 25 January 2004.

3 For the attack of 1994, see above p. 70.

Cesare Previti was condemned to five years' imprisonment for the corruption of the Roman judge Renato Squillante. As we have seen, six months earlier Previti had already received a sentence of eleven years' imprisonment for a similar act of corruption in the case concerning the Mondadori publishing house.[4] In November the judges found Previti not guilty of corruption specifically related to the selling off of the publicly owned food company SME, but of generic corruption relating to Squillante's activities as a judge. On 6 March 1991, the sum of $434,404 had left the 'Ferrido' account of Fininvest at the Credito Svizzero bank of Chiasso, transited fleetingly through Previti's 'Mercier' account in the Darier Hentsch bank in Geneva, and had then been deposited in Squillante's 'Rowena' account in the SBT bank in Bellinzona.[5] The courts have not been convinced by the defence's explanation of why so much money had made its way from a hidden account of Fininvest to the hidden account of a senior Roman judge.

One does not need to have the deductive powers of a Sherlock Holmes to conclude from the evidence presented at these trials that Previti was a trusted intermediary working for Fininvest. However, the owner of Fininvest was not himself implicated. In June 2003, as we know, just as this last trial was reaching its conclusion, he had been granted temporary immunity by his own parliamentary majority and by the President of the Republic.[6] Seven months later, in an unexpected judgement of January 2004, Italy's Constitutional Court decided, by ten votes to five, that the first article of this immunity

4 See above, p. 145.

5 Luigi Ferrarella, 'Previti condannato, ma non per la Sme', *Corriere della Sera*, 23 November 2003. It is perhaps worth reminding readers once again that both the April and November sentences have been passed only at the first level of Italian justice, and that until the Appeal Court and then the Cassation Court pronounce judgement Previti goes free.

6 See above, pp. 145–7, 166–7.

law was in violation of articles 3 and 24 of the Republic's constitution. The law was therefore declared invalid. The judicial pendulum has thus swung once again, at least in part, away from Berlusconi, and his trial for judicial corruption will now be reopened in Milan, though with new judges. Whether or not they will be able to bring the trial to a conclusion is a matter of opinion. The defence will have recourse to all manner of delaying tactics, in the hope that the statute of limitations will once again come into force.

The other area where the centre-right government has been checked concerns the new telecommunications law, approved by parliament on 2 December 2003. The most controversial parts of the law concern concentration of ownership, amounts of advertising, and the assigning of the limited available number of terrestrial frequencies. On the first issue, the new law has taken as its unit of measure the SIC, the integrated system of communications, which covers every part and activity of the communications industry. No single proprietor is supposed to exceed 20 percent of the SIC. However, so large and amorphous is the new body in question, and so controversial the calculation of what one-fifth of it might be, that the possibilities of enforcing a limitation on ownership size are remote indeed. The invention of the SIC has thus been widely interpreted as a means of protecting Berlusconi's media empire and allowing its further expansion. On advertising, the ceiling on publicity will not take into consideration 'telepromozioni', which are the sort of thing much beloved of Italian and American television, where the compère of a variety show and his female aides suddenly interrupt it to start eating a certain type of salame, drinking a certain brand of coffee, or pretending to drive a certain type of car. Television audiences can thus be even further saturated by advertisements. On frequencies, the law simply continues, at least for the moment, the present system, which privileges Berlusconi's three channels, all terrestrial. In so doing it is in open contradiction of various rulings by the Constitutional Court.[7]

On 15 December 2003 the President of the Republic, Carlo Azeglio Ciampi, refused to sign the new law. This was not as bold a gesture as might first appear. Italian presidents have often refused to sign new laws, which then return to parliament for eventual modification. But even if the law is not modified, the President of the Republic has no option but to sign it the second time round. Ciampi's gesture was thus more of a belated warning than anything else, but welcome none the less. Perhaps of equal significance, given its international resonance, was the final report by Freimut Duve, the head of the OECD Office for the protection of freedom of expression in the mass media. Duve issued his report on 11 December 2003, four days before Ciampi's decision, after having served for six years as the first director of an OECD Office 'which has become widely known and respected, and which is constituted by a staff of devoted professionals drawn from half-a-dozen countries'. In a passage worth quoting at length, Duve identified Berlusconi and his friend Vladimir Putin as two notable menaces to the freedom of mass communication:

I have to state here and now that I am leaving the OECD after six years, taking with me an uncomfortable memory. In certain of our member states the present situation regarding the freedom of the mass media is more problematic now than it was when I took up this position in 1997. Who would then have believed that in the development of the new democratic Russia the Cremlin would still have exercised in 2003 direct or indirect control over many newspapers and the totality of the electronic means of information? Who could

---

7 Useful on all this is the recently published book by Carlo Rognoni, *Inferno TV. Berlusconi e la legge Gasparri*, Milan 2003.

have foreseen that the elections which have just taken place for the Duma would have been so widely criticised for their failure to conform to international standards, precisely because of the lack of independence of the means of information? . . . And who then would have been able to predict that the Prime Minister of one of the founder members of the European Union would have promulgated a law on mass communications tailored precisely to foster his own political programme and the economic interests of his family?[8]

~

The Berlusconi government seems to be weighed down by perennial problems – its leader's battle with the judiciary, his conflict of interests, hostile international public opinion, a stagnant economy. In the face of this immobility, the most innovative development in recent months has come not from Berlusconi (unless we wish to judge his face-lift as such), but from Gianfranco Fini, the leader of the National Alliance and Vice-President of the Council of Ministers. In November 2003 the Israeli authorities at last allowed Fini, after repeated requests on his part, to pay an official visit to their country. Fini laid a wreath at the Museum of the Shoah in Jerusalem, and made a number of statements of considerable importance: Fascism had been 'an absolute evil', the anti-Semitic laws of 1938 'infamous', the Salò Republic of 1943–45 'a disgrace'.[9] For someone who less than ten years earlier had called Mussolini 'the greatest statesman of the twentieth century' this was progress indeed. It is also in very marked contrast, as we have just seen, to Berlusconi's grasping of every occasion to minimise the defects of the regime. Fini incurred the wrath of considerable sections of his party, but held steady.

8 www.osce.org. 11 December 2003.

9 Alberto Stabile, 'L'ultimo strappo di Fini', *la Repubblica*, 25 November 2003.

Behind his actions lies a clear desire to establish further his credentials as a moderate, and to prepare a possible succession to Berlusconi. A division of opinion and strategy is beginning to take place in the 'House of Liberties': on the one hand lies the axis which extends from the racist Northern League to the hard-line Treasury Minister Giulio Tremonti, to Berlusconi himself. On the other Fini and the popular former Christian Democrat Pierferdinando Casini, who is the Speaker of the Chamber of Deputies and one of the leaders of the small, moderate Catholic component of the centre-right. It would be an exaggeration to call this a split. All the components of the 'House of Liberties' know that they have nowhere to go if they abandon Berlusconi's protective cover. But the lines for a future battle are being drawn up, and Fini, in spite of his past, wishes to be in a position to extend the appeal of his party to moderate voters.

Meanwhile Berlusconi marches on. Even though the odds are lengthening against him, and more than once he seems tired and even unwell, it would be a grave mistake, as I have argued throughout this book, to underestimate his determination and capacity to recoup. If some reforms are being held up for the moment, such as that on the mass media, others, designed to change the very character of Italy's democracy and its fragile balance of powers, are forging ahead. The autonomy of the magistrates is in the process of being destroyed. The devolution envisaged by Bossi will create a series of regional baronies. The composition of the Constitutional Court is to be changed. The powers of the premier are to be greatly increased, so as to establish his ascendancy not just over parliament but, if need be, over his own majority as well.[10]

The moment of truth will be the spring of 2006, the date of the

10 Giovanni Sartori, 'La maggioranza onnipotente', *Corriere della Sera*, 22 January 2004. The bill in question is no. 2544, and it will shortly be debated in parliament.

next national elections. If Berlusconi wins again, there can be no doubt that he will establish a fully fledged politico-media regime in the heart of Europe. At stake, therefore, is the future of one of Europe's wealthiest and most important countries, a country that is deeply loved for its extraordinary contribution to European civilisation, for the magnificence of its landscapes, and for the spontaneity, intelligence and generosity of its inhabitants. I have tried to explain something about the political, cultural and mediatic battle that is now being waged here, and to argue that its outcome will have more than one implication for the future of international democracy.

Paul Ginsborg
Florence
15 February 2004

INDEX